D1522123

THE PHYSICAL NATURE OF CHRISTIAN LIFE:
NEUROSCIENCE, PSYCHOLOGY, AND THE CHURCH

This book explores the implications of recent insights in modern neuro-science for the church's view of spiritual formation. Science suggests that functions of the brain and body in collaboration with social experience, rather than a disembodied soul, provide the physical basis for the mental capacities, interpersonal relations, and religious experiences of human beings. The realization that human beings are wholly physical, but with unique mental, relational, and spiritual capacities, challenges traditional views of Christian life as defined by the care of souls, a view that leads to inwardness and individuality. Psychology and neuroscience suggest the importance of developmental openness, attachment, imitation, and stories as tools in spiritual formation. Accordingly, the idea that care of embodied persons should be fundamentally social and communal sets new priorities for encouraging spiritual growth and building congregations.

WARREN S. BROWN is Professor of Psychology and Director of the Travis Research Institute at the Graduate School of Psychology, Fuller Theological Seminary. He is a research neuropsychologist with more than eighty peer-reviewed scientific papers on human brain function and behavior. He has also edited or co-authored four previous books, most recently *Neuroscience, Psychology and Religion* (with Malcolm Jeeves, 2009).

BRAD D. STRAWN is Vice President for Spiritual Development and Dean of the Chapel at Southern Nazarene University in Oklahoma. He recently co-edited the book *Wesleyan Theology and Social Science: The Dance of Practical Divinity* (2010), and he is an ordained Elder in the Church of the Nazarene.

The Physical Nature of Christian Life

Neuroscience, Psychology, and the Church

WARREN S. BROWN

BRAD D. STRAWN

CAMBRIDGE
UNIVERSITY PRESS

CAMBRIDGE UNIVERSITY PRESS
Cambridge, New York, Melbourne, Madrid, Cape Town,
Singapore São Paulo, Delhi, Mexico City

Cambridge University Press
32 Avenue of the Americas, New York, NY 10013-2473, USA

www.cambridge.org
Information on this title: www.cambridge.org/9780521734219

© Warren S. Brown and Brad D. Strawn 2012

First published 2012

Printed in the United States of America

A catalog record for this publication is available from the British Library.

Library of Congress Cataloging in Publication Data
Brown, Warren S., 1944–
The physical nature of Christian life : neuroscience, psychology, and
the church / Warren S. Brown, Brad D. Strawn.
p.   cm.
ISBN 978-0-521-51593-1 (hardback)
1. Theological anthropology – Christianity.   2. Psychology and religion.
3. Psychology, Religious.   4. Neurosciences.   5. Religion.
6. Spiritual formation.   I. Strawn, Brad D.   II. Title.
BT701.3.B76   2012
233'.5–dc23   2012002650

ISBN 978-0-521-51593-1 Hardback
ISBN 978-0-521-73421-9 Paperback

Contents

Acknowledgments

Books, and ideas that go into books, do not occur in a vacuum and are seldom completely novel. Books emerge from the interplay of the ideas of the authors interacting with those in other books and in the minds of other persons. What the reader will find in *The Physical Nature of Christian Life: Neuroscience, Psychology, and the Church* emanates from more than a decade of thinking, reading, and talking with other thinkers about the nature of persons and the life of the church. The roots of this work can also be found in articles and book projects that we have been involved in – separately and together – that explored the implications of new scholarship in neuroscience, social science, and Biblical studies. Thus, our book has a conceptual history that we wish to acknowledge.

One of the origins of this project was Warren's sabbatical year (1986) spent with Donald MacKay in the Department of Communication and Neuroscience at Keele University, UK. MacKay was an early participant in conversations about the relationship between neuroscience and Christian faith. This experience helped push Warren out of a comfortable nest formed by what MacKay called "conceptual apartheid," in which science (neuropsychology, in this case) and Christian faith are not allowed to intermingle. MacKay was also a proponent of an embodied view of human nature. Through MacKay, Warren also met Malcolm Jeeves, who was then head of the Department of Psychology at the University of St. Andrews in Scotland. Within the context of a friendship of more than twenty years, Warren and Malcolm collaborated on both scientific papers and science and theology books (most recently Jeeves and Brown, *Neuroscience, Psychology and Religion: Illusions, Delusions, and Realities about Human Nature*, Templeton Press, 2009). Thus, both

Donald MacKay and Malcolm Jeeves have had a significant influence on our thinking about the embodied and embedded nature of humankind.

A pivotal event in the journey toward this book was Warren joining philosopher and Fuller Seminary professor Nancey Murphy, Malcolm Jeeves, and other scholars in an edited volume entitled *Whatever Happened to the Soul? Scientific and Theological Portraits of Human Nature* (Fortress Press, 1998). Warren's chapter in that book was his first foray into writing about cognitive neuropsychology in the context of a theological and philosophical view of persons as bodies, not bodies inhabited by souls. That book project also brought into the conversation New Testament scholar Joel Green (now also at Fuller), who has influenced our perspectives regarding what the Bible has to say about human nature.

Warren and Nancey Murphy extended this earlier project into another book in which they developed a case for human freedom and moral responsibility within the context of this embodied view of personhood. They aimed to defend free will against the assertion that, because we are physical creatures, it must be the case that our behavior and choices are determined by physical laws (Murphy and Brown, *Did My Neurons Make Me Do It? Philosophical and Neurobiological Perspectives on Moral Responsibility and Free Will*, Oxford University Press, 2007). In the context of these projects, Nancey played a significant role in clarifying for us the philosophical context surrounding ideas of human embodiment and the physical basis of mind. In addition, it was during this coauthored book project that Nancey and Warren discovered Alicia Juarrero's important book in philosophy of mind, *Dynamics in Action: Intentional Behavior as a Complex System* (MIT Press, 1999), in which she used the theory of complex dynamical systems (described later in this book) to account for how mind can originate from the processes of the human brain and to suggest important tools for defending the reality of human choice.

Brad and Warren first began collaborating on questions of human nature, psychology, and the church as doctoral student (Brad) and mentor (Warren) in the School of Psychology at Fuller Seminary (while also being members of the same extended family). Besides being mentored by Warren, Brad was also formed as a psychologist through relationships with other Fuller professors, most particularly Winston

Gooden and Hendrika VandeKemp, as well as a core group of his classmates at Fuller. The influence of the late Randall Sorenson was also significant for Brad, as Randy pushed him to pursue analytic training and to develop his thinking about the integration of psychology and Christian faith.

Brad and Warren's research collaboration at Fuller involved study of a telephone-based psychological intervention: 1) for persons at risk of stress-related illness (Strawn, Hester, and Brown, "Telecare: A Social Support Intervention for Family Caregivers of Dementia Victims," *Clinical Gerontologist*, 1998); and 2) as a means of congregational support (Zwart, Palmer, Strawn, Milliron, and Brown, "The Impact of Lay Pastoral Telecare on the Spiritual Well-Being of Church Attenders," *Journal of Pastoral Counseling*, 2000). This project explored empirically the practical and congregational implications of viewing humans as bodies nested in supportive human networks. Brad and Warren continued to collaborate in later years, writing about other topics related to this book (Strawn and Brown, "Wesleyan Holiness through the Eyes of Cognitive Science and Psychotherapy," *Journal of Psychology and Christianity*, 2004; Brown, Marion, and Strawn, "Human Relationality, Spiritual Formation, and Wesleyan Communities," in Armistead, Strawn, and Wright, *Wesleyan Theology and Social Science: The Dance of Practical Divinity and Discovery*, Cambridge University Press, 2010; and Brown and Strawn, "Human Bodies and Church Bodies: Spiritual Flourishing and Formation," in Noth, Morgenthaler, and Greider, *Pastoral Psychology and Psychology of Religion in Dialogue*, W. Kohlhammer, 2011).

Because this is a book about the church (as well as about human nature), Brad and Warren have been influenced by their experiences of life in their churches. For the past seven years, Warren has been involved in planting a new church (Mountainside Communion, Monrovia, CA). This process has included many hours over breakfast or coffee with his pastor, Joshua Robert Smith, talking about the nature of Christian life and the church. In addition to the valuable perspective offered in these conversations, Josh has read and given valuable feedback on early drafts of some of the chapters of this book, providing a more grounded and less idealistic perspective. Also, a number of intelligent and thoughtful members of Warren's congregation read through this book with him and provided important feedback: Eric Bridges, Beth Reisler, Justin Little, Rebecca Pratt, Daniel Lundgren, Brittany Michado, Armen Rashidyan, and Michael Mierzejewski, with occasional help from a few others. In addition, Sonia Luginbuhl graciously allowed us to re-narrate the story she told at a Mountainside worship committee meeting (in Chapter 8). Fly fishing and backpacking are a stimulating part of Warren's life, partly because of the really smart and insightful people he goes fishing with. In the context of these trips, perspectives that have influenced this book have come from Dennis Vogt, Kevin Reimer, Rick Miller, and Warren Brown III (Ren).

Brad has been involved in and nourished by Oklahoma City First Church of the Nazarene. This church clearly exhibits the meaning of embodied Christian life, including caring for whole persons and loving your neighbor as yourself. Brad and his pastor/soul-friend, Jon Middendorf, have also engaged in frequent conversations around the church and "life together." These conversations have provided valuable perspectives for this book. Chris Yates, Brad's friend and church book club leader, gave valuable feedback on an early draft of the manuscript.

A significant contribution to Warren's perspective on Christian life and the church is offered continually by his wife, Janet. However, Janet's most important contribution to the quality of this book was editing every page for correct punctuation, awkward wording, and incomprehensible sentences. We are deeply indebted to her for this incredibly important contribution. We also thank Brad's wife Suzanne for patiently and skeptically listening to, and reflecting on, these "heretical" ideas over the years.

For the sake of the extended family that we share – most particularly Linda, Loren, Suzanne, Evan, Keaton, Janet, Ren, Jenny, Natalie, Caden, Charise, Josh, and Leah – we both pray we will somehow get it right as embodied Christian persons who are deeply embedded in the lives of our family and our church communities.

I

ও

Bodies or Souls?

A MODERN (GNOSTIC) PARABLE

Jeremy was running late for church. He had been out late the night before and had overslept, but he wanted to get there on time to attend his young professionals Sunday School class. Although he did not have many good friends there, he still felt it important as a Christian to be there.

But he could not leave without attending to some urgent business email messages from his accountant. He first checked over the attached financial statements from his small manufacturing business. The picture he saw was a bit worrisome. There was enough money for the month's payroll, but he was still uncertain about sales in the coming months. The email from his accountant recommended that they lay off a couple of people to save money. One of the persons in line to be laid off was a single mom who would be struggling financially without the job. What to do? He quickly made the decision to go ahead. As Jeremy sent the email, he was feeling a little bit sorry to have to do it, but he was trying to run the business on a sound financial basis and did not want to let emotions cloud his judgment.

Driving to church allowed Jeremy time to think about the class discussion he was about to join. His Sunday School class had been talking for several weeks about how to develop a deeper personal relationship with Christ and cultivate a more meaningful spiritual life through prayer and personal devotions. They had even branched into some discussion of contemplative spirituality and centering prayer as ways to cultivate their inner spiritual lives. The thought of this evoked conflicting feelings. On one side, this sounded unrealistic and distant from his daily life (and also a bit "fringy"). On the other side, he was concerned and motivated regarding the state of his spirituality and his soul.

When Jeremy arrived, it was prayer time and the class was sharing requests. One person asked prayer for Roger who was still going through chemotherapy. Jeremy had gotten to know Roger recently through the class and he was glad to have come in time to hear about Roger because he hadn't known that Roger had cancer.

Another person shared that a member of the class named Marcie was worried about losing her job. As the story was told, Jeremy was increasingly drawn into concern for her. Although what was being said suggested that she had been attending for a while, he did not think he knew her ... but somehow the name seemed familiar. Then the name slowly came into focus – he had just sent an e-mail confirming that she would be laid off from his company on Monday.

WHAT DOES IT MEAN TO BE SPIRITUAL?

This fictional vignette illustrates a problem that many of us face. On the one hand, we wish to be more spiritual. In the hope of making some progress, we do things such as going to church, attending retreats, or reading devotional books that we hope will help us cultivate our inner spiritual lives. On the other hand, although we hear a certain amount about Christian love and charity, we have a hard time bridging the gap between our spiritual lives and the demands of day-to-day life. How does spirituality relate to behavior and decisions in our everyday physical and social existence – decisions about business, time caring for friends, or commitment to the church?

Jeremy is a person of orthodox Christian belief. He believes very deeply in God, Jesus, and the Trinity. He believes the Bible is true and attends church faithfully. If you ask Jeremy to define Christianity, he would say it is "a personal relationship with Jesus Christ." Christianity is a spiritual thing – a matter of the heart. Growing in the faith comes about by the renewing of one's heart or mind – meaning that the inner self or soul is made increasingly holy by the Holy Spirit working within one's heart. Jeremy believes that his first-line Christian responsibility is to engage in inward acts of piety, prayer, and Bible study. The ultimate goal for the Christian is for the soul to make it to heaven.

Jeremy would also say that taking care of persons who are homeless, sick, or distressed is an important thing for Christians to do. However, because he believes that faith is an inner spiritual matter, concern for others is regarded as a hoped-for outgrowth of an inner spiritual life. But he finds it difficult to figure out exactly how this happens. What is the relationship between inner spirituality, the routines of daily life, and the physical or social needs of others?

For Jeremy, as for many of us, spirituality is *disembodied*. It is about the state of the soul – a nonphysical thing dwelling inside, but separate from his body and behavior. Thus, his primary focus should be on the state of his soul – everything else is filtered through this individual, inner, disembodied lens. From this perspective, it is hard to get a clear view of the importance of community, or of the priority to be given to caring for those in need.

Generally, most modern religious persons (Christians and non-Christians) believe that spirituality is something that occurs inside themselves and that is experienced individually and privately. Many individuals today hold to this same belief. In part, it is what lies behind the currently popular phrase, "I am spiritual, but not religious," which usually means that the person making the statement does not attend a church or subscribe to a set of denominational doctrines. Such folk do, however, cling to the idea that they can access some kind of spirituality individually and internally, particularly when they are alone in some quiet and aesthetically beautiful place such as the mountains, listening to music, or reading spiritual books.

Christians have always felt in their bones that there is something important about attending church (check out Heb. 10:24–25). But for most of Christian history, the church was thought to be important because the sacraments (offered only by priests) and the experiences of worship (available only in the church) were the only avenues through which a person could encounter God. As modern Christians increasingly forsake such thoughts in favor of individual, inward spirituality, the role of church becomes less and less clear.

Of course, the church itself is not at all clear of its own fundamental value. As church members we often cannot describe in a convincing way why church is important, other than, (1) we get a kind of warm internal feeling from it (suggesting that we are, for the moment, closer to God), and (2) we believe that, through regular attendance, we will somehow grow as a Christian (but we are vague about how this occurs). Pastors tend to view the value of church attendance, at least implicitly, as a context for enlightening parishioners through their preaching. None of these arguments for church have much traction for many in modern culture who believe that spirituality is an entirely inner and private matter.

Thus, in the predominant modern view of spirituality, neither one's physical body, nor other persons, nor church communities, are relevant. Spirituality is both disembodied (that is, manifest in the inner state of the soul, which we experience as emotions and feelings) and disembedded (an entirely individual state not directly relevant to any other person). Spirituality is an inner reality – one that is only distantly related to ourselves as physical/social beings, or to the nature of our relationships with other people or communities.

HAVING A BODY OR BEING A BODY

In this book, we will argue that one's view of *human nature* is critical in understanding the nature of Christian life. What sort of creatures are we? In what way are we to be considered spiritual?

Somehow we Christians have come to believe that we *have* bodies, not that we *are* bodies. We act as if the "real me" is not our own body, or even our own behavior, but is something spiritual (not physical) inside – our mind or soul. Thus, it is considered possible to be spiritual inside without being religious in what we do – without participating in a communal religious life. We believe we can be good persons inside, even though we are often inconsiderate, unethical, or even immoral in what we do.

But there are events and experiences that directly assault this idea. As Christian theologian and ethicist Stanley Hauerwas tells us, "Sickness makes it impossible to avoid the reality of our bodies. When I am sick, I am not a mind [or soul] with a suffering body; I am the suffering body."[1]

---

[1]   Stanley Hauerwas, "The Sanctified Body: Why Perfection Does Not Require a 'Self'," (1999), 29, in S. M. Powell and M. E. Lodahl, eds., *Embodied Holiness: Toward a Corporate Theology of Spiritual Growth*, (Downers Grove: Intervarsity Press, 1999), 19–38.

When we are racked with the aches and pains of the flu, or half delirious with fever, we are pretty sure that we are a body. If, because of an auto accident, a friend is brain damaged, and his or her mental capacities, personality, or behavior is dramatically changed, we realize ever so clearly that we are a body.

The issue regarding whether humans are composed of a body and a soul, or are simply a body, has a long history in philosophy and theology. We called the story above a Gnostic parable as a reference to the heresy called Gnosticism that plagued the early church. Gnosticism held that humans are souls trapped in fleshly, sensual, and sinful material bodies, existing in a corrupt and polluted material world. To be spiritual we must escape from the impact of both our bodies and this imperfect world. In order to escape and free ourselves from the influence of the material body and world, we need to obtain special spiritual knowledge (*gnosis*, in Greek) through a direct (mystical) experience of the transcendent world of the spiritual. Combating the impact of this heresy on the development of Christian faith was a major focus of New Testament writers, particularly in the Gospel of John and the letters of Paul.

Very generally, the idea that humans are composed of two parts – a material body and a nonmaterial soul (or mind) – is called *dualism* (indicating a dual or two-part human nature). The alternative, that we are only bodies, is called either *monism* (indicating a single, unified nature) or *physicalism* (emphasizing the physical constitution of humankind). Monism asserts that human nature is *embodied*, in that all that we are as persons involves characteristics emerging from our bodily makeup. We believe there is much to be said in favor of this view and a great deal to be learned about Christian life by considering its implications. The intent of this book is not to present a convincing argument in favor of monism-physicalism, although we will present a glimpse of the rationale for this position. Rather, we wish primarily to explore what it would mean for Christians, and for the church, if this were true – that we are physically embodied.

However, human nature cannot be entirely explained by our embodiment. It is also critical to take into account the social embeddedness of persons. Since our brains are highly malleable in response to situations – which we commonly call learning – our ongoing interactions with our social world continually and progressively shape and reshape who we are as persons. Thus, a rich account of human nature also requires an account of the impact of families, social relationships, groups (churches), and cultures.

The idea that humans are physically embodied beings can be problematic if not properly understood. Some have argued that the idea that human beings are bodies, not souls inhabiting bodies, implies that the rules and laws of atoms, molecules, or basic biology entirely determine all of human life. If this were in fact the case, it would make free will impossible and all human relationships meaningless, because everything in human life and experience would be nothing more than physics and biology. Such a view could not stand the scrutiny of Christian theology.

However, others (ourselves included) have proposed that the idea that human beings are bodies does not necessarily lead to this conclusion.[2] That is, due to the incredible complexity of bodies, new properties emerge in human and animal life that transcend, but do not eliminate the rules operating on atoms, molecules, and basic biology. So, we believe a very convincing case can be made that humans have very high level properties that emerge from biology that endow them with the capacity to think, make decisions, relate meaningfully to one another, and to know and love God. In this context, being "soulless" is not the same as being a physiological robot without human feelings and experiences, without free will, and incapable of genuine love.

Some believe that the idea that humans are bodies (not souls occupying bodies) is problematic from the point of view of scripture. In what follows, we will deal with the issue of a scriptural understanding of human nature with respect to bodies and souls. However, beyond this, we do not intend to review and critique all of the philosophical and theological arguments for and against dualism or monism.[3]

---

[2]   Warren S. Brown, *Whatever Happened to the Soul? Scientific and Theological Portraits of Human Nature*, ed. Warren S. Brown, H. Newton Malony and Nancey Murphy, (Minneapolis: Fortress Press, 1998).

[3]   For the reader interested in the issue of monism versus dualism, we recommend books by Joel Green, Nancey Murphy, and N. T. Wright, among others, cited throughout this book and found in the Resources section at the end.

WHAT IF WE ARE BODIES?

This book is about bodies – human bodies and church bodies. We hope to show not only the critical implications for Christian life of the bodily nature of humans, but also how much this view can deepen our faith, enrich the life of the church, and allow us to grow as Christian persons. It really makes a significant impact on the way we think about Christian life if the essence of a human person is not a ghostly, immaterial substance (such as a soul or spirit or mind) that is temporarily trapped in a fleshy body. We believe that we are simply bodies, but made and designed that way by God. We want to explain how this idea really matters for how we live our lives and how we understand and participate in the church.

When, like Jeremy, we believe that spirituality is about something inside of us that is separate from our body, we have good reason to focus our attention on the state of our soul and to be less attentive to our actions as whole persons in the world. We also have good reason not to be overly concerned – perhaps just mildly concerned – about the physical, social, or economic distress of other persons. However, if we are wholly a body, we must think differently about the nature of Christian life. We must focus our attention outward toward God rather than inward toward our own soul. *Spirituality* would be understood as an ongoing relationship with God who is spirit, but outside of the person, and not as the cultivation of a particular form of experience inside of the person. Christian life would not be about the inner "me," but about a bodily person in relationship to that which is outside of the person – God, my neighbor, and the community of believers.

If we are wholly bodies, we also would need to think differently about our life together in the church. We have to reconsider why we need the church. The primary activity of the church would not be saving souls or fostering inner spirituality. Rather, church would be about redeeming persons from a life focused on themselves (even on their own spirituality) to participating in a life focused on what God calls the church to be and do in the world. The goal of church would be to become a community – a closely interrelated network of physical persons – that could itself come to function as the embodied presence of Christ in the world. Members of the body would come into relationship with Christ and grow primarily through the Spirit being manifest in ongoing interactions with other Christians within the church.

A SUMMARY OF WHAT IS TO COME

This book will describe the nature of embodied human life and relate this view to what we believe should be the nature of Christian formation, community, and the church. The book is divided into three parts:

In Part I we set the stage by focusing on the issues of dualism in Christian faith. We argue that the origins of body-soul dualism are mostly in Greek philosophy and that this view of human nature has been read into scripture, rather than taken from scripture. In Chapter 2, we also give a brief look at how the church came to be mostly dualist and to the issue of Gnosticism in both the early church and in modern understanding of spirituality and Christian faith. In relationship to this historical and scriptural background, we summarize in Chapter 3 some of what is currently known about the physical basis of human nature and human life – that is, the neurological basis of mental processes, inter-personal relationships, moral decisions, and religious experiences.

Part II begins with a description of the principal forces that govern our mental and social development during infancy and childhood, resulting in the formation of our personality and character as discussed in Chapter 4. Our focus is how physical human beings become *persons*, in the richest sense of that term, and that the critical forces in the development of personhood are social and interpersonal. We are not only embodied (physical beings), but also *embedded* in human communities. Chapter 5 considers how the forces that shape child development continue to shape us as adults, allowing for the possibility of continued growth in wisdom and Christian maturity. Finally, in Chapter 6 we describe how persons can change and be transformed in their personhood, even in the face of inadequate prior social development. In general, this part of our book describes what embodiment implies for understanding the development of persons and the continuing process of maturity and formation.

In Part III we consider what it would mean to take seriously our embodiment and the processes of human formation and change described in Part II in the context of the church. Thus, we attempt to translate these perspectives on human beings as bodies into an understanding of the nature of the body of Christ – the church. We focus particularly on the dynamic interactions and influences between persons and communities. Chapter 7 makes the argument from the perspective of forces that contribute to the formation of mature Christians. How do the social and interpersonal forces inherent in communities work toward the continued formation of Christian persons? Why do embodied persons need to be embedded in the church? Chapter 8 considers the church itself as a network of persons. How do we understand the church as a body? How do churches form and reform into that which can increasingly become the Body of Christ in a very literal sense? Chapter 9 highlights the critical role of the narratives that are explicitly told or implicitly manifest in the church as they form the body that is the congregation. As an example of how narratives form imagination and action, this chapter takes up issues of disability and dependence as they are encountered within the church. Chapter 10 serves as a recap of our entire argument. There we summarize the points we have tried to make throughout the book to provide readers a concise review. Here we also explicitly differentiate our views from others that readers might assume are implied, but that we clearly do not mean to endorse or imply.

Thus, this book raises issues with far-reaching implications for Christian life. Do we minister to immaterial souls or to embodied whole persons? How are people formed and how do they change? What does it mean to be spiritual? How should the church conduct itself so as to be maximally transformative to those who participate? How is the Body of Christ to respond to persons within its community with physical, mental, economic, or psychological needs and disabilities? What should be the church's response to injustice in the world?

We hope that in reading this book, you, our reader, will begin to have a new appreciation for Christian persons as *whole-embodied-persons-embedded-in-the-church*. With this view in mind, you can come to better understand the processes of personal and spiritual development, maturity, and change, as well as the processes involved in the growth of a church into a Body of Christ. Perhaps you will begin to rethink, as we have, the nature and the mission of the church with respect to its call to foster the Christian formation of persons, to be continually formed into a genuine Body of Christ, and, ultimately, to be transformative in its influence on the wider community in which it exists.

ɑᴠ

HUMAN NATURE AS PHYSICAL

PROSPECT

We begin our exploration into the implications of a more wholistic and embodied understanding of persons for Christian life and the church in Chapter 2. We first describe briefly and thus somewhat simply the philosophical, historical, and theological background of body-soul dualism. In evaluating this view of human nature, it is important to know where it came from. Thus, we give a short history of the philosophical origins of body-soul dualism. We argue that the origins of body-soul dualism are mostly in the philosophy of Plato, with contributions and elaborations by St. Augustine in early Church history, and by René Descartes during the Enlightenment. We also argue that body-soul dualism is not the view of the Bible. Along with many biblical scholars, we believe that body-soul dualism has been taken as an *a priori* premise and read into scripture, rather than being the view we learn from scripture. Historically, dualism has also had a strong influence on the church in the form of the heresy of Gnosticism fought by the early church fathers. However, versions of Gnostic spirituality have hung around the church throughout the centuries, including a strong influence of this form of spirituality in modern religious life.

In relationship to the philosophical, historical, and scriptural background of Chapter 2, we summarize in Chapter 3 recent research in neuroscience and clinical neurology that lends strong support for viewing human nature as physical and embodied. We particularly focus on studies of the functioning of the brain with respect to what seem to be uniquely human capacities. We organize this discussion along the lines of attributes of human nature that, at various times in the past, have been presumed to be the exclusive domain of the soul and the capacity that makes humankind distinct from animals: rationality, relationality, morality, and religiousness. In each case, we find phenomena of brain disorders described in clinical neurology, and research studies involving brain scans in normally functioning individuals that make a strong case that these properties of humanness are not the result of having a non-material soul, but are the outcome of the functioning of a highly complex brain.

Once we have set the stage in Part I concerning the origins of body-soul dualism and the evidence suggesting that this view may not be the best way to think about humankind, we venture in Part II into discussions of human development and change. In Part III, we present our views on Christian formation and the life of the church that flow out of these perspectives.

Christian History and the Two-Part Person

MINI VIEWS

Gary bought a new Mini Cooper. He considered himself to have purchased an economy car that would save significantly on gas. Consequently, he drove his Mini to conserve fuel – no jackrabbit starts from stop lights, reasonable freeway speeds, cautious cornering, and use of the six-speed manual transmission to keep the engine RPMs low. Rod also bought a Mini, but Rod was attracted by the fact that the Mini was built by BMW, had a turbocharged engine, great gearing, racing suspension, and regularly won rally competitions. Obviously, Rod drove his Mini much differently than Gary. He enjoyed its sports-car acceleration, loved moving dramatically through the gears, and was turned on by fast runs over curvy mountain roads. While Rod's test drive in the Mini had reminded him of the Alpha Romero Giulia Spider he had owned in the 1960s, Gary considered his Mini to be a reincarnation of his 1966 VW bug.

VIEWS OF OURSELVES

The way we view and understand a thing has a significant impact on how we interact with it. This truism is not limited to cars, but applies equally to our view of ourselves and other persons. Looking at ourselves through different philosophical lenses has different implications for action.

If each of us is a combination of a physical body and a nonmaterial spiritual soul, then we "drive this car" with one thing in mind – primarily the nurturing and preservation of our inner immortal soul. [The car metaphor works well here – the "real me" is the driver inside controlling the action of the car and experiencing the thrill.] However, if we are entirely a physical body – albeit a body with incredible cognitive, social, and spiritual capacities – then we would drive that sort of car differently. Since "me" and "my body" refer to the same integrated whole, there is not a separate inner thing to be concerned about and which is presumed to be responsible for driving the car. [That is, the metaphor of driving a car is no longer apropos.] From this view, we are wholly integrated physical beings focused on life in the world outside of us – both material and spiritual.

For most of its history, the Christian church has been dominated by the view that persons have a dual (two-part) nature – body and soul. This *dualism*, as it is called, asserts that humans are composites of two different parts, a material body and a nonmaterial spiritual soul. These two parts are not equals in that the soul is considered to be superior to the body and to rule over it. In addition, the soul is immortal, while the body is mortal and transitory. Of course, this concept has implications for how we conduct ourselves and how we view others (that is, how we interact with this sort of "car"). If the soul is superior to the body and rules over it, then we must focus our energies on caring for and nurturing our soul first and foremost. Only after our soul is given its due are we obligated to seek the spiritual welfare of the souls of others. Finally, if time and energy permit, we can allow ourselves to pay attention to our own body and outward behavior or to be concerned about the physical, economic, and social well-being of other persons.

HOW CHRISTIANS CAME TO BE DUALISTS

In order to better comprehend an idea that has become deeply ingrained in our thinking by its cultural predominance, it is helpful to review its history. Where did this idea come from? Body-soul dualism has a complex history. We can simplify this history by pointing to three historical figures – all philosophers – who famously championed the idea: Plato, St. Augustine, and Descartes.

The Greek philosopher Plato (BC 428–348) taught that the world available to our senses was only a reflection – a mere shadow – of the real world of eternal forms. Every physical thing that we see or touch is only a manifestation of the real thing that exists in the eternal world of ideal forms. This idea applied to people as well as to trees and rocks. For Plato, there was a difference between our physical bodies and the real person who existed in some other nonmaterial realm. Thus, Plato was the first prominent philosopher to champion the idea of a nonmaterial aspect (form or soul) that was more important and real than the physical. We have all learned how Greek ideas filtered through the Mediterranean world during the time of the Roman Empire. Greek culture was so prominent in Palestine in the time of Jesus that the New Testament was written in Greek. Greek words would tend to be associated with Greek ideas, at least in the minds of some early readers.

St. Augustine of Hippo (354–430) was heavily influenced by the ideas of Plato. Augustine's contribution to Christian dualism was to link the two-part view of human nature (body and soul) with a reformulation of Christian spirituality that turns attention inward toward the status of the soul. This form of *inwardness* assumes that the essential "me" is inside (the soul), and that one's body is merely a temporary vessel whose sinful passions are to be controlled by the soul. Since the soul is spiritual, it is superior to the body, and therefore must rule over the body. For Augustine, and much of the Church since his time, spirituality is the cultivation of an inner and introspective life, with the body given lesser regard when considered in relation to the really essential and important part of the person – the inner, nonmaterial soul. Besides turning our attention inward, this formulation of personhood also fosters *individualism* – each person focused on, and solely responsible for, his or her own soul.

During the Enlightenment, philosopher René Descartes (1596–1650), heavily influenced by Augustine, is credited with solidifying the sharp distinction between the body and the soul (or mind, which Descartes considered the same as the soul). The medical physiology of the ancient Roman physician, Galen of Pergamum (129–ca. 200), was still dominant in Descartes's time. Galen taught that the body was inhabited by many souls. In this view, there was a soul for the heart, and one for the brain, and one for the liver, and souls that made muscles contract. Descartes contradicted this earlier view by arguing that all of these basic bodily functions were aspects of a physiological machine, and that the functioning of animals did not transcend these mechanisms. The problem for Descartes was imagining how such a biological mechanism could result in human consciousness, will, and rationality. He solved this problem by retaining *one* soul in his philosophy of human nature. Thus, humans were considered to be unique with respect to animals in having a nonmechanistic immaterial rational soul – but only one. According to Descartes, what it means to be human is to have inside the body a "thinking thing," and the inner processes of this rational thinking thing were believed to be the foundation of all rational knowledge, including knowledge of one's own existence and of God.

The dualism of St. Augustine, and later of Descartes, became dominant in Christian theology and persists to the present time in the following common assumptions: possession of an inner nonmaterial soul is essential to our humanness; the body is secondary and its passions are to be ruled over by the soul; the foundation of all knowledge is the rational capacity of the soul (or mind); spirituality is the cultivation of the inner life; and we have free will only as the soul rules over the body, which is otherwise a physiological machine.

WHAT THE BIBLE TEACHES ABOUT HUMAN NATURE

Over the past one hundred years or so, much emphasis in biblical studies has been on the effort to recapture the original meaning of the texts of the Bible. The presupposition of this endeavor is that, over the two-plus millennia since biblical times, secular cultural views have come to strongly influence our understanding of what is being conveyed by the stories and teachings of the Bible. In the process of this reexamination of scripture, scholars have carefully looked at the idea that the Bible teaches that humans are a composite of a body and a soul.

Strongly influenced by Plato, Augustine, and others, it was for many centuries the dogma of the established church that body-soul dualism was clearly supported in the Bible. However, many biblical scholars have come to the conclusion that dividing persons into a body and a soul is not a view that can be found in scripture. Many now believe that dualism has been read into, rather than derived from, scripture. Nevertheless, a dualist reading of scripture has a tenacious grip on the way many Western Christians read the Bible. As biblical scholar N. T. Wright put it, "We have been buying our mental furniture for so long in Plato's factory that we have come to take for granted a basic ontological contrast between 'spirit' in the sense of something immaterial and 'matter' in the sense of something material, solid, physical."[1]

Particularly important in understanding a scriptural view of human nature is the Genesis 2 account of the creation of humankind. Many have read into this passage the idea that when God breathed into Adam the breath of life (*nephesh*), this amounted to giving Adam a soul – a special nonmaterial thing not possessed by animals. The Hebrew word *nephesh* was translated as *psyche* in the Septuagint and then into English as *soul*. Some passages from the King James Version seem to fit nicely into a body-soul dualism.

Psalm 16:10:   "For thou wilt not leave my soul in Hell."

Psalm 49:14–15:   "Like sheep they are laid in the grave; death shall feed on them; and the upright shall have dominion over them in the morning; and their beauty shall consume in the grave from their dwelling. But God will redeem my soul from the power of the grave: for he shall receive me."

While these passages appear to indicate that the body is something that will die and decay and the soul is something that is separate, immaterial and immortal, other passages seem to contradict this dualist perspective.

Psalm 7:1–2:   "O Lord my God in thee do I put my trust: save me from all them that persecute me, and deliver me: Lest he tear my soul like a lion, rending it in pieces, while there is none to deliver."

Psalm 22:20:   "Deliver my soul from the sword."

In these latter passages, it sounds as if it is the soul that can be damaged or destroyed by physical processes![2] Much of the problem lies in the fact that the Hebrew word *nephesh* has many possible meanings, including life, person, breath, desire, self, and even throat.[3] Given the weight of

---

[1]   N. T. Wright, *Surprised by Hope: Rethinking Heaven, the Resurrection, and the Mission of the Church* (New York: Harper One, 2008), 153–154.

[2]   See Nancey Murphy, *Bodies and Souls, or Spirited Bodies?* (London: Cambridge, 2006) for further discussion of these passages.

[3]   See Joel B. Green, *Body, Soul and Human Life: The Nature of Humanity in the Bible* (Grand Rapids, MI: Baker Academic, 2008), 54.

increasing evidence, modern translations have increasingly used words other than soul to render the meaning of *nephesh*.[4]

Diogenes Allen argues that in the creation account God does not breathe a soul into a human, but the human becomes a *nephesh* – a living being. "Thus in the Bible, we do not *have* a soul we are souls, that is, living beings."[5] On lexical grounds alone this term *nephesh*, translated as psyche or soul, is best understood as referring to the whole person rather than some part – which is why most scholars believe the Hebrews understood humans to be physical and indivisible.[6] However, as Allen and others believe, the point is not crystal clear in the Bible because the Bible is not interested in giving a detailed anthropology of the human person (monist, dualist, or tripartite), but rather gives a description of human relatedness to God, one another, and all of creation.

Similarly, theologian LeRon Shults argues that the account of human creation makes it clear that humans are embedded in God's physical creation and "no special part of humanity, not even the mind, escapes this creaturely continuity."[7] Biblical scholar Joel Green provides a some-what different emphasis, arguing that humans are described as both continuous and discontinuous with the creation of animals. We are continuous in our physical embodiment. We are discontinuous in that God establishes a particular form of relationship with humankind – a relatedness that constitutes the image of God. "Only to humanity does God speak directly"[8] – and this speaking involves vocation. Green summarizes the view of human nature in Genesis as follows:

Genesis does not define humanity in essentialist terms but in relational, as Yahweh's partner, and with emphasis on the communal, intersexual

---

4 For example, all four passages from the Psalms are translated as "me" rather than "my soul" in the New International Version.
5 Diogenes Allen, "Persons in Philosophical and Biblical Perspective," in Malcolm Jeeves, ed., *From Cells to Souls – and Beyond: Changing Portraits of Human Nature* (Grand Rapids, MI: Eardmans, 2004), 165–178.
6 Joel Green, "What Does it Mean to Be Human? Another Chapter in the Ongoing Interaction of Science and Scripture," in Malcolm Jeeves, ed., *From Cells to Souls – and Beyond: Changing Portraits of Human Nature* (Grand Rapids, MI: Eardmans, 2004), 179–198.
7 F. LeRon Shults, *Reforming Theological Anthropology: After the Philosophical Turn to Relationality.* (Grand Rapids, MI: Eerdmans, 2003), 164.
8 Joel B. Green, *Body, Soul and Life Everlasting.* (Grand Rapids, MI: Baker Academic, 2008), 62.

character of personhood, the quality of care the human family is to exercise with regard to creation as God's representative, the importance of the human modeling of the personal character of God, and the unassailable vocation of humans to reflect among themselves God's own character.[9]

Thus, throughout the Old Testament persons are viewed as a unity – as physical beings that are part of God's physical creation, but standing in a unique vocational and covenantal relationship with God.

In addition, most biblical scholars believe that the Gospels also do not teach or imply body-soul dualism. Of course, distinction regarding bodies and souls that some might read into the Gospel texts rests on Greek words, yet Jesus spoke in Aramaic and thus it is impossible to know if the teaching of Jesus presumed any form of body-soul dualism. The few Gospel passages that might be read in a dualist manner (e.g., Matt 10:28) are at best ambiguous and, many believe, are best read from a nondualist perspective.[10]

Consensus is less clear with respect to the New Testament Epistles, although here again many scholars have come to the conclusion that even the epistles are best understood as presuming persons to be undivided and physical. Those few passages in Paul's letters that seem to imply a body-soul distinction are interpreted by many Bible scholars as Paul simply co-opting the language of the day to make important points about Christian faith, but in these passages he was not presuming, nor intending to teach, a body-soul distinction. Most importantly, the primary focus of scripture is a narrative of God's redemptive acts in history, not an explanation of human nature. Therefore, the issue of the nature of human persons is not directly addressed.

In his book *The New Testament and the People of God*, theologian N. T. Wright helpfully clarifies the various possible meanings of the term *dualism* within Christian thought and biblical discourse.[11] He provides a useful list of ten different dualities that are important to consider in

---

[9] Ibid., 65.

[10] An nondualist exegesis of Matt 10:28 and other passages can be found in Joel Green, "Three Exegetical Forays into the Body-Soul Distinction," *Criswell Theological Review* 7, no. 2 (Spring, 2010), 3–18. Similar exegesis of other passages can be found in Joel Green, *Body, Soul and Life Everlasting* (Grand Rapids, MI: Baker Academic, 2008).

[11] N. T. Wright, *The New Testament and the People of God* (Minneapolis: Fortress Press, 1992), 252–253.

theology, some of which are fundamental to Christian doctrine. For example, the theological dualities that distinguish between God and his physical creation and between good and evil are core Christian beliefs. Two other dualities that Wright describes are of particular concern to us. The first is *cosmological dualism*, the idea that the physical world is secondary and shabby, compared with what can be experienced by the mind or spirit. This is the view of Plato, described earlier, that the physical world that we see is a mere shadow of the reality that exists in the nonmaterial realm of form. The second is *anthropological dualism*, the idea that humans are composed of a body and a soul arranged in a hierarchy – soul ahead of body. Examples of this form of dualism can be found in the writings of St. Augustine and René Descartes. These latter two forms of duality Wright considers "definitely marginal" with respect to our understanding of the New Testament, classifying them as pagan, by which he means that they come from non-Christian sources, such as Greek philosophy.

One of the reasons that this definitely marginal belief in a body-soul distinction has persisted in Christian thinking is that it seems to provide a ready explanation for life after death – the body dies and the soul goes to heaven. However, this idea does not appear to be consistent with New Testament teaching. The core message of the New Testament is not that our souls fly off to heaven at death, but that our bodies are transformed and resurrected. For example, Jesus, after his resurrection, goes to great lengths to emphasize his *bodily* presence, albeit a transformed body. He is clearly not a disembodied spirit. "Look at my hands and my feet. It is I myself. Touch me and see; a ghost [that is, a disembodied soul] does not have flesh and bones, as you see I have." (Luke 24:39 New International Version: NIV; our bracketed interpretation). As New Testament scholar Joel Green puts it, "In Luke's report of Jesus' post-resurrection existence, we find no witness to resurrection as escape from bodily existence . . ., nor is it possible to confuse Jesus's postmortem existence with that of an angel; his, rather, is a transformed materiality, a full bodily resurrection."[12] Thus, the Christian hope is for resurrection in a transformed body.

---

[12] Joel B. Green, "Resurrection of the Body: New Testament Voices Concerning Personal Continuity and the Afterlife," in Joel B. Green, ed., *What about the Soul? Neuroscience and Christian Anthropology* (Nashville: Abington Press, 2004), 92.

Defenders of the idea that body-soul dualism is the view of the Bible often point to the Apostle Paul's comments in II Corinthians 5:1–6:

For we know that if the earthly tent we live in is destroyed, we have a building from God, an eternal house in heaven, not built by human hands. Meanwhile we groan, longing to be clothed instead with our heavenly dwelling, because when we are clothed, we will not be found naked. For while we are in this tent, we groan and are burdened, because we do not wish to be unclothed but to be clothed instead with our heavenly dwelling, so that what is mortal may be swallowed up by life. Now the one who has fashioned us for this very purpose is God, who has given us the Spirit as a deposit, guaranteeing what is to come. Therefore we are always confident and know that as long as we are at home in the body we are away from the Lord. [NIV]

When read through modern glasses already tinted with body-soul dualism, this passage seems to suggest something about the soul (the "real me") being trapped in an "earthly tent" and that, being trapped "in the body," we are "away from the Lord." But New Testament scholar Joel Green and other biblical scholars believe that a correct reading of this passage must take into account Paul's more complete discussion of the resurrection of the body in I Corinthians 15: 35–58. Here Paul emphasizes two forms of bodily existence – an earthly body that is corruptible and perishable (being progressively destroyed by persecution, suffering, or old age), and a transformed, incorruptible, imperishable, resurrected, heavenly body that can dwell with God and inherit the kingdom of God. In both states, we are bodies. Thus, with respect to the passage from II Corinthians quoted above, Green concludes, "[T]his passage provides no warrant for disembodied, human existence . . . ."[13] as would be the case if our souls left our bodies at death to be with the Lord.

The sharp contrast between the dualism of St. Augustine and Descartes and the view of human nature found in the Bible is also asserted by philosopher Diogenes Allen. Allen writes, "The Bible, rather than making the 'material' and the 'spiritual' polar opposites, as in Descartes' contrast of the material and the immaterial, stresses that the

[13]   Joel Green, "What Does it Mean to Be Human? Another Chapter in the Ongoing Interaction of Science and Scripture," in Malcolm Jeeves, ed., *From Cells to Souls – and Beyond: Changing Portraits of Human Nature* (Grand Rapids, MI: Eardmans, 2004), 192.

spiritual aspect of our person is our relation to God and all that God has created, both human and nonhuman. The contrast of 'flesh' and 'spirit' that we find in Paul's letters is not a conflict between body and mind; rather 'flesh' represents all that is at war with God's will in our person, including our minds, which can be 'fleshly'."[14]

DUALISM IN THE EARLY CHURCH

Even before St. Augustine, the early church struggled against Christian faith being corrupted by heretical doctrines. Chief among these heresies was Gnosticism – a religious movement throughout the Mediterranean world, with roots in Greek philosophy, that taught that humans are divine souls (or spirits) trapped in a material body and material world. While the soul is divine and good, the physical body and the material world are imperfect and evil. Biblical scholar Raymond Brown, in his *Introduction to the New Testament*, describes the major tenants of Gnosticism as follows: ". . . human souls and spiritual principles do not belong in this material world. . . . [Human souls] can be saved only by receiving the revelation that they belong in a heavenly realm of light . . . Ascent to this realm is sometimes through baptism, sometimes through elaborate cultic rituals (often involving anointing), sometimes more through philosophical reflections."[15] Thus, for Gnostics, the goal of human life is to free oneself from the inferior material body and the outer material world by gaining *special spiritual knowledge* (that is, gaining gnosis).

Christian Gnostics viewed Jesus as a divine spirit or Supreme Being who came to earth to bring gnosis (an understanding of the heavenly realm) in order to free souls from being entrapped in human flesh. Because the material body was evil, Christian Gnostics believed that Jesus could not have had a physical body. The early church considered these Gnostic beliefs to be heretical. Against this heresy, John writes in his gospel, "The word became flesh and made his dwelling among us."

[14] Diogenes Allen, "Persons in Philosophical and Biblical Perspective," in Malcolm Jeeves, ed., *From Cells to Souls – and Beyond: Changing Portraits of Human Nature* (Grand Rapids, MI: Eardmans, 2004), 167.

[15] Ramond E. Brown, *An Introduction to the New Testament* (New York: Doubleday, 1997), 92.

(John 1:14 NIV) The impact of pagan Gnosticism on the views of many early Christians is an example of how our views of our selves and of the Gospel can be influenced or altered by other ideas and worldviews that gain cultural popularity.

Understanding the Gnostic heresy is important because it persists in current religious thinking as the conceptual framework of body-soul dualism. We will be referring, throughout this book, to the Gnostic tendencies deeply rooted in modern Christian thought and practices and in the daily life of the church.

THE GNOSTICISM OF CONTEMPORARY CHRISTIANITY

The inward focus on the soul, fostered by dualism, creates a strong magnet drawing modern religious perspectives almost inevitably toward Gnosticism. Many consider modern Western Christianity to be essentially Gnostic. Harold Bloom writes in his book *The American Religion*: "... the real American religion is and has always been in fact ... Gnosticism. ... It is a knowing by and of an uncreated self ... and [this] knowledge leads to freedom ... from nature, time, history, community, and other selves ..."[16] In Bloom's view, our belief in an uncreated, nonmaterial self (or soul) frees us from concern for the natural world, current events or history (our own or that of our community), or the lives of other persons. Such problems are of no compelling concern to a non-material soul.

Lines from an old gospel song come to mind as an illustration of Gnostic influences in modern expressions of Christian faith:

> *This world is not my home, I'm just a'passin through.*
> *My treasures are laid out somewhere beyond the blue.*
> *The angels beckon me through heaven's open door;*
> *and I can't feel at home in this world anymore.*

While for some people life on this earth is indeed hard, many of the folk who have sung this spiritual over the years have meant that this world and this physical body are inherently evil and corrupt, and therefore "not

---

[16] Harold Bloom, *The American Religion: The Emergence of the Post-Christian Nation* (New York: Simon and Schuster, 1992), 49.

my home." The "real me" is a soul that belongs in heaven. One's soul is just passing through this world, temporarily trapped in a body like a bird in a cage. That is, a person (one's soul) does not belong to the materiality of this world, and yearns to escape to the heavenly realm.

Another by-product of dualism is the primacy of the inner: the soul that is believed to reside inside individual persons is of first concern. In recent years books aimed at helping Christians focus on and enhance the inner spiritual life have been particularly popular. About this genre of Christian literature, theologian Owen Thomas comments,

> In the tradition of writing about the Christian life or spirituality, commonly known as ascetical theology, down to the present burgeoning of this literature, a pervasive emphasis and focus has been on the inner or interior life as distinct from the outer, bodily, and communal life. . . . My thesis . . . is that this emphasis is mistaken philosophically, theologically, and ethically.[17]

Thomas believes that the modern Christian emphasis on inwardness poses

> . . . one of the greatest paradoxes of Christian history. On the one hand, the biblical tradition seems to emphasize the primacy of the outer – the bodily, speech and action – while, on the other hand, the Christian tradition under the influence of . . . Augustine and Dionysius, among others, tends to emphasize the inner.[18]

Thomas' concern is the ethical problem created when the goal of the moral life is the perfection of the soul. Virtue and moral behavior become a means to an end – an end that is heavily tainted with inwardness and individualism.

A further problem with dualism is that inwardness comes coupled with individuality – ultimate concern for one's own soul at the expense of ethical behavior toward other persons and toward God's creation. Wendell Berry, in his essay "The Body and the Earth,"[19] points out the prevalence and negative impact of what he refers to as a "separation of the body from the soul." This is a fundamental property of Gnosticism.

---

[17] Owen Thomas, "Interiority and Christian Spirituality," *The Journal of Religion* 80, no.1 (2000).

[18] Ibid., 51.

[19] Wendell Berry, "The Body and the Earth," in Wendell Berry, *Recollected Essays* (San Francisco: Northpoint Press, 1981).

As Berry describes it, we consider our bodies to be mere shopping carts for busing around our souls, and this belief affects our understanding of our lives as Christians and as persons within communities. The following is a paragraph in which Berry elaborates this point in fairly sharp language:

For many of the churchly, the life of the spirit is reduced to a dull preoccupation with getting to Heaven. At best, the world is no more than an embarrassment and a trial to the spirit which is otherwise radically separated from it. The true lover of God must not be burdened with any care or respect for His works. While the body goes about its business of destroying the earth, the soul is supposed to wait for Sunday, keeping itself free of earthly contaminants. While the body exploits other bodies, the soul stands aloof, free from sin, crying to the gawking bystanders: "I am not enjoying it!" As far as this sort of "religion" is concerned, the body is no more than the lusterless container of the soul, a mere "package" that will nevertheless light up in eternity, forever cool and shiny as a neon cross. This separation of the soul from the body and from the world is no disease of the fringe, no aberration, but a fracture that runs through the mentality of institutionalized religion like a geologic fault. And this rift in the mentality of religion continues to characterize the modern mind, no matter how secular or worldly it becomes ... And yet, what is the burden of the Bible if not a sense of the mutuality of influence, rising out of an essential unity, among soul and body and community and world?[20]

In the remainder of his essay, Berry makes a strong case for a chain of negative consequences of this separation of the life of the body from the more important status of the soul. "Contempt for the body," he says, "is invariably manifested in contempt for other bodies – the bodies of slaves, laborers, women, animals, plants, the earth itself." Berry also links this modern Gnostic contempt for the body to a romanticizing and instrumentalizing of sex, weakening of marriages and households, breakdown of communities, and finally to a disrespect for God's physical creation and the environment.

Christian ethicists Glen Stassen and David Gushee, in their book *Kingdom Ethics*, discuss the negative impact of dualism and its emphasis on inwardness on Christian ethics. Not mincing words, they write, "To

---

[20] Ibid., 283–284.

the extent that Christians adopt any kind of body/soul, earth/heaven dualism we simply do not understand the message of Scripture – or of Jesus."[21] Later in the book, Stassen and Gushee specify clearly what they mean by this statement, and what they believe are the consequences of dualism for ethics:

> One classic tendency in Christian thought has been the development of a thoroughgoing *dualism* in which sharp dichotomies are drawn between body and spirit/soul, world and church, law and gospel, and so on. The tendency of this kind of theology has been to identify God with the former (spirit, church, gospel) and expel or radically alter the nature of God's presence in the latter (body, world, law). The goal of the church is to rescue souls from bodies, rescue the church from the world, and transport its passengers safely to the heavenly realms. The implication for ethics has tended to be a lack of emphasis on obeying the teachings of Jesus in real physical, this-worldly life . . . .[22]

Thus, the Christian church, strongly influenced by the dualism of St. Augustine and René Descartes, became heavily invested in the distinction between body and soul. The individualism and inward focus fostered by dualism has led the church into a progressive resuscitation of Gnosticism – Christian life is to be lived in the spiritual realm, disconnected from every day bodily life and community interactions.

Gnostic ideas also became an important source of the emergence of secular nonreligious spirituality in the late twentieth century. Subscribers to this view seek a unique inner spiritual experience that is affective, subjective, disembodied, and unrelated to their physical existence in the world, their actions, their relationships with other persons, or any particular religious community. These folk often say, "I am spiritual, but not religious" – which is a thoroughly Gnostic statement.

Like the differing views of a Mini Cooper held by Rod and Gary that resulted in different styles of driving the same make of car, what we believe to be the nature of our selves and other persons has a great deal to do with how we live each day, interact with others, worship, pray, and participate in the life of the church. Is the "real me" a soul trapped in a

---

[21] Glen H. Stassen and David P. Gushee, *Kingdom Ethics: Following Jesus in Contemporary Context* (Downers Grove, IL, Intervarsity Press, 2003), 28–29.
[22] Ibid., 115.

body longing to escape? If so, then Christian spiritual life must be experienced and lived in the inner realm of our soul or spirit. However, if a person is entirely a body within God's physical creation, then spirituality is a matter of the quality of one's relationship to God and his Kingdom (outside of "me"), and therefore a matter of one's physical life and behavior as it occurs within the context of interpersonal relationships, the fellowship of the church, participation in the sacraments and acts of worship, and those actions that lead to the redemption of the lives of other persons.

As we go forward, we intend to explore with you, our readers, the implications of these different views for the life of Christian persons, congregations, and communities (in Part III). However, before setting forth on this exploration, we will describe some important aspects of the physical embodiment of persons about which we must be clear before we can appropriately understand individual and corporate Christian life. Therefore, we need now to delve into the wondrous world of our neurological embodiment – the human brain.

3

∾

Embodied Soulishness

THE VISIONS OF SISTER JOHN

Sister John opened a fresh notebook and began to write. Adoration welled up through the pain, closing of the gap between lover and Beloved. The force of his presence curved eternity in on itself; it was not her love rising after all, but his love pulling her toward him. She fell upward into brilliance, where all suffering was released.

In the fire of his embrace, all that was her ceased to exist. Only what was God remained.

[some days later, Sister John interacting with the Mother Superior]

Dear God, help me bear this –
"Are you sure you're all right, dear? You look very pale."
"Forgive me, Mother . . ."
The notebook fell off her lap.
have mercy

She was sure the blood vessels in her head would give way. . . . .
Her mind fractured under the pressure. She splintered like a broken glass . . . she was sure this had to be death, it had to be the end of everything, then her suffering blinked off.

an invisible sun
a shock wave of pure Being
swept my pain away, swept everything away
until all that was left was God.

[the diagnosis from Sister John's physician]

"The EEG showed that you have an epileptic disorder, but so far the seizure activity is localized in the temporal-lobe area of the brain. That's good – it's kept you from having grand-mal attacks, the kind that spread across the whole brain and cause convulsions. Temporal-lobe seizures tend to be more psychological."

From Salzman, *Lying Awake*[1]

VISIONS AND THE BRAIN

Mark Salzman, in his novel *Lying Awake*, tells the story of Sister John of the Cross, a nun in a Carmelite convent in Los Angeles. As described in this passage, Sister John experiences powerful and overwhelming religious visions. These visions came to mark her as an important spiritual resource, both within and outside her community – perhaps a saint. However, as the story progresses, it becomes clear that her visions are a product of epileptic seizures. The dilemma that provides the drama within Salzman's narrative revolves around whether to undergo a surgery that will "cure" the seizures, but will also eliminate her wonderful and luminous spiritual visions.

The religious experiences associated with the epileptic seizures of Sister John are consistent with the accounts of religious experiences provided by a small portion of patients with temporal lobe epilepsy when describing their seizures. We will deal more thoroughly with the issues of seizures and religious experiences later in this chapter. However, this story raises the deeper question about the relationship between spirituality and bodily existence. In what sense are our deepest and richest spiritual experiences associated with the normal or abnormal functioning of the brain? Certainly, within the conceptual and religious world of St. Augustine and René Descartes (as we encountered it in the previous chapter), it is hard to resolve this dilemma. Of all things, religious experiences should be spiritual and not physical.

This chapter aims to briefly describe some of the evidence from brain research (also referred to as *neuroscience*) that demonstrates that the highest and most distinctive characteristics of human nature are the outcome of the functioning of our bodies and brains and are no longer easily assigned to a nonmaterial soul or mind. All of the human

[1] Mark Salzman, *Lying Awake* (New York: Alfred A. Knopf, 2000), 17, 36–37, 68.

characteristics that at various times in history have been presumed to be the exclusive domain of the soul have been found to be outcomes of bodily processes. Our intention in this chapter is to reinforce the conclusion that it is not necessary that we have a soul in order for us to be rational, relational, moral, and religious beings. These capacities emerge from the functioning of an incredibly complex brain-body.

In the history of Christian thought, there have been four human capacities that have been thought to define the unique contribution of the possession of a soul to the nature of humankind: *rationality, relationality, morality*, and *religiousness*. In what follows in this chapter, we will summarize some recent studies of the human brain that focus on these four "soulish" characteristics of persons. The primary point of this brief review of neurology and neuroscience is to make even clearer the physical embodiment of all that we are. The eventual target is to gain an understanding of the physicality of human nature so that we can think in a more adequate way about the life and ministry of Christian persons and congregations. Ultimately, our aim is not for the comprehension of abstract information, but for the development of greater practical wisdom about Christian life.

RATIONALITY

As we saw in the last chapter, René Descartes postulated the existence of a non-material soul because he could not imagine how rationality – that is, uniquely human intelligence – could be a product of bodily processes. Bodies were thought to be merely mechanical or hydraulic systems, and such systems are not rational. However, three centuries of clinical observations of persons with brain damage or disease, and research regarding the functions of the brains of humans and animals, have made it rather clear that (1) rationality and intelligence are the product of the activities of the brain, and (2) the unique power of human intelligence is related to larger brains and particularly distinctive brain processes.

The relationship between brain function and the various cognitive capacities that go together to make up intelligence and rationality is obvious to anyone who has witnessed the consequences of stroke. Brain damage due to stroke can cause disruption or elimination of various mental abilities, such as loss of the capacities for language (speech, writing, or reading), mathematical ability, memory, planning, spatial thinking (e.g., finding one's way around the neighborhood), drawing, recognizing visual objects, or even recognizing the faces of members of one's own family. Each of these rational capacities can be disrupted in relative isolation by a stroke affecting small areas of the cerebral cortex of the brain but can also be disrupted more generally and progressively in a brain disorder such as Alzheimer's disease. In addition, failure of normal brain development, or brain damage prior to or after birth, can lead to mental retardation or more specific forms of mental disability.

Research on brain function in human beings has rapidly advanced in the past few decades due to the emergence of technology that allows one to see brain structure and function in a conscious living person. Magnetic resonance imaging (MRI) allows scientists and physicians to look at the structure and integrity of brain tissue inside the skull in a gray-scale image like an x-ray. Using *functional* MRI (fMRI), it is possible to superimpose on the brain structure seen in an MRI an additional representation of brain areas that have relatively higher metabolic activity during any particular form of mental processing (typically represented by color patches superimposed on gray-scale MRI pictures). By this method, patterns of brain activity can be observed during a mental state or while accomplishing a specific cognitive task.

Brain scans of persons without brain disorders have more than reinforced the findings from brain damaged patients. The cerebral cortex (the wrinkled outer layer of the upper part of the brain) is the critical organ for rational thought. For example, fMRI studies show that brain activity increases (that is, "lights up" with color on fMRI images) in specific areas of the left side of the cerebral cortex when a person is asked to do a simple language task, such as provide verbs to accompany nouns. Somewhat different but overlapping areas of the left cerebral cortex are active when a person listens to someone else talk. A different pattern of areas of the cerebral cortex are active when a person is involved in solving mathematical problems; yet another pattern occurs when one is trying to negotiate a path through a complicated environment in a video game. Other areas light up when a person is planning an action he or she might do. However, when the action being planned has interpersonal consequences, additional areas of the brain become active.

What is important about the finding of unique patterns of brain activity during particular forms of thinking is that it becomes clear that each form of rational mental activity is based on a unique pattern of activity across the surface of the cerebral cortex (as well as patterns of activity in brain areas below the cortex called subcortical structures). Different forms of rational thought are due to different patterns of brain activity. Stroke or other forms of brain damage disrupt critical nodes and junctures in these neural networks and, therefore, result in deficiencies in various mental abilities.

In today's world, relationships between brain damage or patterns of activity in brain scans and rational thought seem unproblematic – we take it as a matter of course. However, three centuries ago, Descartes did not have access to what is known in modern neurology. Thus, he could not imagine how it could be that matter – that is, physical bodies and brains – could do anything rational or intelligent. So he concluded that these human capacities must be due to a nonmaterial thing. Descartes referred to this nonmaterial rational thing as the "mind" or "soul." Given the continuing influence of St. Augustine (particularly on Descartes himself), this rational soul became wedded to ideas about the inner realm of spirituality. However, in the modern world of rapidly advancing understanding of the role of the brain in rational and intellectual capacities, the *rational* capacity of a person can be understood as the outcome of patterns of activity in our very large and sophisticated brains, not as a disembodied mind or soul within us.

RELATIONALITY

Within contemporary Christian theology there is a great deal of discussion about the relationality of God. This theology puts particular emphasis on the interrelationships that exist between the three persons of the Trinity.[2] The idea of the relationality of God leads to the further proposal that relationality is what is referred to in Genesis when it speaks of humankind being created "in the image of God." Thus, it has been assumed by some that the reality of a soul is manifest in relationships – between God and persons, and between different persons. Alternatively,

---

[2] Colin E. Gunton, *Christ and Creation* (Grand Rapids, MI: W. Eerdmans, 1992).

we can explore whether the human ability for interpersonal relationships is the outcome of the functioning of our brains and bodies.

The idea that relationality is a distinctive feature of humankind has been proposed within scientific discussions of human nature. Evolutionary psychologist Andrew Whiten studies the social behavior of monkeys. From this perspective, he has theorized that what distinguishes humankind from the rest of the animal world is "a deep social mind."[3] Whiten's claim is "that humans are more social – more deeply social – than any other species on earth, our closest primate relatives not excepted." He continues, " . . . by 'deep' I am referring to a special degree of cognitive and mental penetration between individuals." Given the fact that monkeys are remarkably social in comparison with most other animals, this is a very significant endorsement of the unique relationality of humankind. Whiten also argues that these deep and rich forms of human interpersonal relatedness are dependent on a basic set of human mental capacities. These capacities include language, the ability to understand the mental life of other persons (called a Theory of Mind), forethought (contemplating the social consequences of behavior), and deeper forms of emotional attunement to other persons. While chimpanzees can be shown to possess at least rudimentary forms of these capacities, each is markedly enhanced in human beings.

Currently, the fastest growing domain of neuroscience is social neuroscience – the study of the brain's role in social interactions. Research in social neuroscience is all about the embodiment of human social relations. Thus, a brief review of some of the findings in social neuroscience helps us appreciate how much of our deep social mind is due to the functioning of our brain and body.

Within the fields of neurology and psychiatry, there are disorders of social interactions that are clearly related to brain disorder. A notable example is damage to the midline portion of the frontal lobe of the brain (between the eyes, just behind the forehead). Damage to this area can result in changes in the person's capacity to regulate his or her behavior with respect to either moral standards or normal social conventions, or to take into account the

[3]   Andrew Whiten, "The Place of 'Deep Social Mind' in the Evolution of Human Nature," in M. A. Jeeves, ed., *Human Nature* (Edinburgh: The Royal Society of Edinburgh, 2006), 207–222.

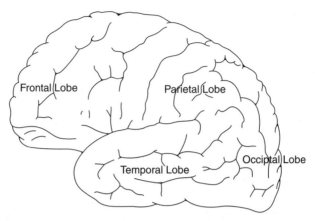

Side View of the Brain (front to the left)

FIGURE 3.1.

well-being of other people. These individuals are markedly capricious in their interpersonal and social behavior. There is also a form of Alzheimer's disease that specifically attacks the frontal lobes and can, as the disease progresses, have a similar impact on social behavior.

Another disorder that has a severe impact on social behavior is autism. Individuals with autism are socially disengaged and don't seem to recognize the personhood of others. In Asperger's syndrome (at the high-functioning end of the autism spectrum), individuals are without an understanding of the mental and emotional life of others and, therefore, are socially inept. Schizophrenia (particularly paranoid schizophrenia) also has a major impact on an individual's relationality. While the physiological causes of autism and schizophrenia are not yet clearly understood, it currently seems most likely that these disorders, with their deficiencies in social relatedness, are caused by either abnormal brain neurochemistry or abnormal brain wiring.

A large number of recent studies in social neuroscience have used techniques of brain imaging (fMRI) to demonstrate the patterns of brain activity that are inherent in different forms of social behavior and social experience in normal individuals. A very clear and important example is the research on empathy. In one study, participants brought a close friend to the testing session. While participants were in the fMRI scanner, an arrow indicated on each trial whether the participant's own hand was about to receive a mildly painful electric shock or whether the friend's hand would be shocked. It was found that the subjective experience of empathy for the friend's impending discomfort triggered a very similar pattern of activity within the emotional systems of the participant's brain that occurred when the participant received the shock. Thus, interpersonal empathy is based on mirroring the emotional experience of the other person's pain within your own brain.[4] When experiencing empathy for another person, brain research suggests that it is at least partially correct to say, "I feel your pain."

Neuroscientists have also used brain imaging methods to study the development of trust. These studies look at brain activity while persons are engaged in playing economic games with another person. During one such game, trust of the other person is measured by willingness to give money to the other person as an investment. The trusting response (or not) is based on the prior history of the other player's willingness to return a reasonable portion of the profits from previous investments. Development of trust in the other player, at least with respect to a willingness to continue to invest, was related to a specific pattern of brain activity, including a brain center involved in anticipation of rewards.[5] Even more intriguing was the finding that when players were given a dose of the hormone oxytocin, there was an increase in the likelihood of behavioral expressions of trust (but this also increased the likelihood of being gullible, as you might imagine).[6] Another study showed that judgments that a person is *not* trustworthy, based on a picture of the face, was related to increased activity in a brain area known to be involved in the experience of fear.[7] So, trust and distrust are constituted by the occurrence of identifiable changes in brain activity, and these behaviors can be modified by the administration of a hormone that has a direct effect on the brain.[8]

---

[4] Tania Singer et al., "Empathy for Pain Involves the Affective But Not Sensory Components of Pain," *Science* 303, no. 5661 (2004):1157–1162.

[5] B. King-Casas et al., "Getting to Know You: Reputation and Trust in a Two-Person Economic Exchange," *Science* 308, no. 5718 (2005):78–83.

[6] P. J. Zak, R. Kurzban, and W. T. Matzner, "The Neurobiology of Trust," *Annals of the New York Academy of Science* 1032 (2004):224–227.

[7] J. S. Winston et al., "Automatic and Intentional Brain Responses during Evaluation of Trustworthiness of Faces," *Nature Neuroscience* 5, no. 3 (2002):277–283.

[8] Somewhat tongue-in-cheek, we might translate "Trust in the Lord with all your heart" into " . . . with all your brain" – except that these trust-related brain systems are interacting with autonomic systems that regulate and monitor heart rate.

A fundamental aspect of our capacity for relationality is the ability to understand the mental states of other persons, which is called a Theory of Mind. To respond appropriately in social contexts, we must infer the intentions, emotions, and mental states of other persons based on their actions or speech. Persons with autism are thought to have a deficiency in this "mind reading" capacity. To study this ability, one ingenious experiment used videos involving animated geometric figures (two moving triangles) to assess the ability of both autistic and nonautistic individuals to attribute mental processes to the triangles as the causes of their movements and interactions. Nonautistic persons inescapably see the interactions of the triangles as depicting interpersonal intentions (such as coaxing, hiding, or teasing) and emotions (such as surprise, fear, or affection), whereas individuals with autism seem only to perceive two triangles in motion. Most importantly, investigators were able to show that the inference of interpersonal (actually, intertriangle) emotion and intentionality from the interactive movements of the triangles over the computer screen involved activation of the middle part of the frontal lobes and parts of the temporal lobes (a part of the cerebral cortex lying just above the ears).[9]

If humans differ from other primates in having a deep social mind, as Whiten argues, what might account for this difference with respect to brain structure? Recent research has proposed one relatively distinct human enhancement in brain wiring that may be critical to our remarkable relational capacities – the proliferation of a special kind of nerve cell called Von Economo neurons. Named after the neuroscientist who discovered them, these neurons are very large and have very long branches (axons) reaching throughout the cerebral cortex. One place of origin of Von Economo neurons is an area deep within the brain that receives information about the visceral state of the body, such as those involved in our body's emotional responses (such as changes in heart rate or blood vessel dilation in blushing, etc). Another adjacent area where these neurons originate is a brain system that is involved in decision making in uncertain conditions. Both of these areas have been found in brain imaging studies to be markedly active during states of empathy or shame, when detecting the mental and emotional states

---

[9] Fulvia Castelli et al., "Autism, Asperger's Syndrome and Brain Mechanisms for the Attribution of Mental States to Animated Shapes," *Brain* 125, no. 8 (2002):1839–1849.

of others, and while making moral decisions. Therefore, it has been hypothe-sized that information about bodily emotional activity is detected in these brain areas, and then this information is spread throughout the cortex by Von Economo neurons. Information distributed by these neurons provides a way of regulating our thinking according to our bodily states and emotions (our "gut feelings").[10] Integration of thinking with information about bodily states is important for signaling the social significance of our actions and perceptions, providing us with the mostly unconscious feelings that modu-late our social behavior.

The importance of the Von Economo neurons to our consideration of the source of the deep social mind of humankind is the fact that these neurons are relatively unique to humans. They are found in great abundance in the adult human brain, but they are few in number in chimpanzees and gorillas, and entirely nonexistent in lower primates.[11] Small numbers of these neurons are also found in a few other highly social animals (such as elephants and some species of whales and dol-phins). Most interestingly, these neurons are few in number in newborn human infants but are already as numerous as in adults in the brain of a four-year-old child. Thus, it is assumed that the progressive development of these neurons is critical for the burgeoning of social capacities as infants grow into children.

From these neurological cases and the blossoming of research in the neuroscience of human social abilities and social interactions, it is clear that human relational capacities are not to be consigned to the possession of a nonmaterial soul, but, like rationality, they are the outcome of the functioning of our large and uniquely constructed brains. The deep social mind of human beings is due to the incredible capacity of our brains (and bodies!) to process social information in deep, complex, and subtle ways. It has been speculated that it is the unique human capacity for inter-personal relatedness that best captures the richness of the idea that

---

[10] J. M. Allman et al., "The Anterior Cingulate Cortex: The Evolution of an Interface between Emotion and Cognition," *Annals of the New York Academy of Science 935* (2001):107–117. Also, K. K. Watson et al., "Brain Activation during Sight Gags and Language-Dependent Humor," *Cerebral Cortex* 17, no. 2 (2007):314–324.

[11] E. A. Nimchinsky et al., "A Neuronal Morphologic Type Unique to Humans and Great Apes," *Proceedings of the National Academy of Science USA* 96, no. 9 (1999):5268–5273.

persons *are* "souls."[12] For example, when we attempt to bring to mind what it is like to be a soul, we tend to focus our attention on our deepest experiences of relating to God or to one another.

MORALITY

Within Western traditional thought, the soul is also considered the source of all moral behavior. In support of the dependence of morality on the human soul, many argue that morality is the characteristic that is most uniquely human and not found in other animals. So, we need to consider the relationship between our bodies (and brains) and our capacity for moral thinking and moral behavior. To the degree that morality is rational and/or relational, the descriptions in the preceding sections regarding the embodiment of these attributes are certainly relevant and give us some initial perspective.

Over the centuries, philosophers have argued about whether moral behavior is primarily a product of conscious reasoning and deliberation or an expression of unconscious moral emotions and intuitions. That is, does a person consciously contemplate a particular decision with respect to explicit moral principles (such as, "What is best for most people?" or "What does duty demand?") and then act? Or, does a person respond more immediately on the basis of "gut feelings" about what seems to be the right thing to do? Obviously, we all do some of both. The real question is, which of these forms of moral guidance is most reliable, and which should we trust? What is the role of emotions in moral decisions? We do not intend to answer these important questions, but rather to evaluate the role of the body in various forms of moral arbitration and behavior.

For St. Augustine and René Descartes, morality consisted of the immaterial rational mind (also referred to as the soul) controlling the material passions of the body, which were considered to be inherently resistant to moral actions. Thus, the passions (emotions and motivations) of the body needed to be willfully controlled. This dualistic view of

---

[12]   Warren. S. Brown, "Cognitive Contributions to Soul," in *Whatever Happened to the Soul? Scientific and Theological Portraits of Human Nature*, ed. Warren S. Brown, Nancey Murphy, and H. Newton Malony (Minneapolis: Fortress Press, 1998), 99–126.

morality as the mind or soul controlling bodily passions (anger, violence, lust, greed, gluttony, etc.) continues to have a strong influence on Christian thinking about morality.

In earlier research studies, the contribution of moral reasoning versus moral intuition was often studied by proposing moral dilemmas and observing how people solved them. Recently, this method has been enhanced by having persons contemplate moral dilemmas while their brain activity is being scanned. The questions of interest are: (1) What brain systems are being used to process the dilemmas? and (2) What other forms of human mental activity are most similar to the process of making a moral decision? Using fMRI techniques, Harvard psychologist Joshua Greene and his collaborators attempted this sort of investigation. In one study they observed which brain areas increased in activity as participants moved from solving easy moral dilemmas to solving more difficult dilemmas. They found that activity increased in the lateral parts of the frontal lobes, probably due to greater rational deliberation, but activity also increased in the areas of the cortex involved in recognizing and regulating emotions.[13] Thus, both forms of processing (rational and emotional) seemed to be involved.

In another study by the same authors, two different forms of a difficult moral dilemma were presented to individuals who were in the scanner: Would you cause one person to die (hit by a trolley car) in order to save the lives of five others? In one version of the dilemma, the option involved indirectly harming one person by throwing a switch to divert the trolley to save five people, but allowing the death of one. In the other version, the scenario required the participants to decide whether or not they would push one person in front of the trolley to stop it (direct harm to another) in order to save the lives of 5 others. When the participants imagined these two forms of moral choices, their brain showed two different patterns of activity. Decisions about whether to inflict harm *directly* on someone to save five other persons activated more intensely the brain areas involved in the control of social action by our emotions.[14]

---

[13] J. D. Greene et al., "The Neural Bases of Cognitive Conflict and Control in Moral Judgment," *Neuron* 44, no. 2 (2004):389-400.

[14] J. D. Greene et al., "An fMRI Investigation of Emotional Engagement in Moral Judgment," *Science* 293, no. 5537 (2001):2105-2108.

While it is interesting to know how persons solve moral dilemmas, it is uncertain whether such abstract rational processes have anything to do with on-the-ground moral behavior. The term *moral intuitions* refers to moral actions or assessments that occur automatically (without thinking), which are particularly critical in complex situations where one must act quickly. Such intuitions often guide behavior in ways that are not explicitly conscious. Thus, to the degree that a particular behavior is guided by such intuitions, it occurs without (or at least prior to) moral reasoning and deliberation. But are such decisions better? With respect to complex non-moral decisions (such as which car to buy), recent research has suggested that quick intuitive decisions are very often better than decisions made after considerable rational deliberation.[15] This is likely also to be the case for moral decisions required in very complex situations.

The important role of emotions in moral intuitions was argued in a recent influential book by Antonio Damasio entitled (interestingly) *Descartes' Error*.[16] For Damasio, Descartes erred by presuming that emotions are irrational and need to be controlled by reason. Damasio, a neurologist, described individuals with damage to the lower middle portions of the frontal lobes (that area behind the forehead, between the eyes). One of the clinical outcomes of disease or damage to this area of the brain is unconventional and capricious behavior, including an inability to use moral guidelines or social norms in making decisions about what to do or not to do. Most importantly, a series of laboratory studies of these individuals showed that the primary problem was an inability to use feedback from their own bodily *anticipatory emotional responses* to guide decision making. Thinking about a potential action creates anticipatory emotions in us that help us evaluate the consequences of the action being contemplated. Without this feedback from the emotional reactions of their bodies, these patients are set adrift and are no longer anchored by implicit social and moral norms. When asked about moral questions (such as the trolley car dilemma discussed earlier), these individuals respond on the basis of mere calculation regarding how many

---

[15] A. Dijksterhuis et al., "On Making the Right choice: The Deliberation-without-attention Effect," *Science* 311, no. 5763 (2006):1005–1007.

[16] Antonio Damasio, *Descartes' Error: Emotion, Reason, and the Human Brain* (Boston: Norton, 1994).

might be killed, without also being affected by the interpersonal emotions involved in contemplating actually pushing another person to their death.[17] Persons who sustained damage to these same areas of the frontal lobes in early life show psychopathic behavior as adults – that is, they behave without the guidance of conscience and have little ability to control their behavior based on its impact on the well-being of others.[18]

To the degree that intuitions are important to moral behavior, it is important to know how they form. Generally, the degree to which persons are more or less moral in their emotions, intuitions, and automatic behaviors is mostly determined in childhood by the learning and shaping of behavior via direct feedback (rewards and punishments), moral instruction, and the learning of culturally formative stories (narratives about the moral behavior of others). We will discuss these developmental processes in greater depth in the next chapter.

The brains of humans and very intelligent and social animals such as chimpanzees are quite similar, particularly so with respect to the brain systems involved in social emotions. Thus, it is not surprising that some recent research has focused on the precursors of moral behavior in monkeys and chimpanzees. Among the moral sentiments that have been observed in great apes are: social rules, cooperation and mutual aid, sympathy, reciprocity, altruism, and conflict resolution. However, in each case, these capacities and behaviors are very rudimentary compared to those seen in humans. That which is unique about human morality may be the ability to apply foresight, judgment, and reason to the modulation of these moral sentiments. The proliferation of Von Economo neurons in humans compared to apes (described earlier) strongly suggests greater capacity to use feedback from emotions (signals of moral intuitions) to moderate the more rational decision-making processes of the cerebral cortex.

RELIGIOUSNESS

While chimpanzees are relational creatures with very rudimentary moral sentiments (suggesting that relationality and moral emotions are not

---

[17] M. Koenigs et al., "Damage to the Prefrontal Cortex Increases Utilitarian Moral Judgements," *Nature* 446, 7138 (2007):908–911.

[18] S. W. Anderson et al., "Impairment of Social and Moral Behavior Related to Early Damage in Human Prefrontal Cortex," *Nature Neuroscience* 2, no. 11 (1999):1032–1037.

entirely unique to humankind), it is clear that religiousness is distinctively human. In addition, most people consider religious experiences to be a convincing manifestations of the existence of the soul. Spiritual experiences are presumed to be a matter of this inner life of the non-material "me" (the soul) and quite distinct from one's material life and bodily existence.

We began this chapter by relating the story of the epilepsy-related spiritual visions of Sister John of the Cross from Mark Saltzman's novel. A similar account is given in Russian novelist Fyodor Doystoyevsky's book *The Idiot*. In the following passage, Doystoyevsky describes the thoughts of Prince Myshkin as he ruminates about his epileptic seizures.

... he fell to thinking that in his attacks of epilepsy there was a pause just before the fit itself ... when it seemed his brain was on fire, and in an extraordinary surge all his vital forces would be intensified. The sense of life, the consciousness of self, were multiplied tenfold in these moments, which lasted no longer than a flash of lightning. His mind and heart were flooded with extraordinary light; all torment, all doubt, all anxieties were relieved at once, resolved in a kind of lofty calm, full of serene, harmonious joy and hope, full of understanding and the knowledge of the ultimate cause of things.[19]

Doystoyevsky, who himself had epilepsy, goes on to consider, in the thoughts of Myshkin, what might be the meaning of such experiences.

Thinking about this moment afterward, when he was again in health, he often told himself that all these gleams and flashes of superior self-awareness and, hence, of a "higher state of being" were nothing other than sickness, the upsetting of the normal condition and, if so, were not the highest state of being at all but on the contrary had to be reckoned as the lowest. And yet he came finally to an extremely paradoxical conclusion. "What if it were sickness?" he asked himself. "What does it matter if it is abnormal intensity, if the result, if the moment of awareness, remembered and analyzed afterward in health, turns out to be the height of harmony and beauty, and gives an unheard-of and till then undreamed-of feeling of wholeness, of proportion, of reconciliation, and an ecstatic and prayerlike union in the highest synthesis of life?"... If in that second – that is, in the last lucid moment before the fit – he had time to say to himself clearly and consciously: "Yes, one

---

[19] Fyodor Dostoyevsky, *The Idiot*, trans. Henry and Olga Carlisle (New York, Signet Classic, 1969), 245–246.

might give one's whole life for this moment!" then that moment by itself would certainly be worth the whole of life.

In this passage, it is hard to escape the impression of a tight relationship between a deeply religious experience of ecstasy and spiritual awareness and the functioning of the brain (in this case, abnormal functioning associated with a seizure).

The literary descriptions of both Salzman and Doystoyevsky are very similar to the seizure-related experiences of a small portion of individuals with what a neurologist would diagnose as *temporal lobe epilepsy*. Descriptions of temporal lobe seizures found in neurology journals and textbooks confirm that these literary passages give a fairly accurate account of the sort of religious experiences that sometimes accompany a temporal lobe seizure. For example, a patient was reported in the modern neurology literature as describing her seizures in similarly religious tones: "Triple halos appeared around the sun. Suddenly the sunlight became intense. I experienced a revelation of God and of all creation glittering under the sun. The sun became bigger and engulfed me. My mind, my whole being was pervaded by a feeling of delight."[20]

Such clinical reports have led one neuroscientist to speculate regarding the possible existence of a "God module" in the brain – that is, "dedicated neural machinery in the temporal lobes concerned with religion."[21] However, others provide a more limited interpretation. They argue that the emotion systems within the temporal lobe tag certain encounters as "crucially important, harmonious, and/or joyous, prompting comprehension of these experiences within a religious framework."[22] When these structures become abnormally active during a seizure, the resulting subjective experience is sometimes interpreted by the patient as religious. Thus, the perceptual and emotional experience associated with the seizure is interpreted *after the fact* as religious (or not), depending on the prior knowledge, life experiences, and beliefs of the individual who

---

[20] H. Naito and N. Matsui, "Temporal Lobe Epilepsy with Ictal Ecstatic State and Interictal Behavior of Hypergraphia," *Journal of Nervous and Mental Disease* 176, no. 2 (1988):123–124.

[21] V. S. Ramachandran et al., "The Neural Basis of Religious Experiences," *Society for Neuroscience Conference Abstracts* (1997):1316.

[22] J. L. Saver and J. Rabin, "The Neural Substrates of Religious Experience," *Journal of Neuropsychiatry* 9 (1997):498–510.

had the seizure. Whatever the most appropriate statement of the meaning of these seizure-related phenomena, it is clear that certain patterns of electrical activity involving the temporal lobes can in some patients cause intense, personally significant experiences that some persons describe as religious.

One researcher claims to have induced religious experiences by electromagnetic stimulation of the right temporal lobe of non-epileptic persons. Some participants who received the electromagnetic stimulation reported experiencing a sense of presence that was sometimes attributed to the presence of God or angels or ghosts.[23] But here again, not everyone in this research had experiences that they interpreted as religious, so it may be an interaction between the brain stimulation and an interpretation given to the experience (out of the prior conceptual and experiential world of the participant) that makes the event religious.

Unusual, if not abnormal, activity in some of the same brain areas can be elicited by certain drugs. The association between imbibing certain plant substances and the occurrence of religious experiences was not uncommon in ancient religions. These substances were known to facilitate ecstatic and mystical states. For example, the Aztecs used mushrooms and the indigenous peoples of Mexico and the American Southwest used peyote cactus in religious ceremonies. The common subjective experiences elicited by such hallucinogenic substances include: , "altered perception of reality and self; intensification of mood; visual and auditory hallucinations, including vivid eidetic imagery; ... distorted sense of time and space; enhanced profundity and meaningfulness; and a ubiquitous sense of novelty."[24]

---

[23] M. A. Persinger and F. Healey (2002). "Experimental Facilitation of the Sensed Presence: Possible Intercalation between the Hemispheres Induced by Complex Magnetic Fields," *The Journal of Nervous and Mental Diseases* 190 (2002):533–541; M. A. Persinger, "The Neuropsychiatry of Paranormal Experiences," *Journal of Neuropsychiatry and Clinical Neuroscience* 13(2001):515–524. That the experiences are due to suggestion not directly to the brain stimulation was demonstrated by P. Granqvist et al., "Sensed Presence and Mystical Experiences Are Predicted by Suggestibility, Not by the Application of Transcranial Weak Complex Magnetic Fields," *Neuroscience Letters* 379, no. 1 (April 29, 2005):1–6.

[24] A good summary of this information can be found in David E. Nichols and Benjamin R. Chemel, "The Neuropharmaology of Religious Experiences: Hallucinogens and the Experience of the Divine," in Patric McNamare, ed., *Where God and Science Meet: Vol. 3: The Psychology of Religious Experience* (Westport, CT: Praeger, 2006), 1–34.

Precisely how such drugs act on the brain to bring about their hallucinogenic effects is not yet entirely known. However, based on what is known of the brain systems involved and the nature of the changes created by the drugs, such drugs appear to "perturb the key brain structures that inform us about our world, tell us when to pay attention, and interpret what is real."[25] Whether these experiences are interpreted as a so-called psychedelic trip or as a spiritual and transcendent experience is most likely due to the person's expectations, the setting in which the drugs are taken, prior life experiences, and the theological commitments out of which the person provides a post hoc interpretation of the experience.

An example of the impact that hallucinogenic drugs can have on religious experiences is found in the famous Good Friday experiment done many years ago by Walter Pahnke as his Harvard doctoral dissertation.[26] In this experiment, a group of students were given either a placebo or a hallucinogenic drug (psilocybin) – without them knowing which – just prior to listening to a Good Friday service from the basement of a church. Both groups were interviewed immediately after the service and six months later. The group that was given the hallucinogenic drug rated their experiences during the service as significantly more intense and mystical than the group without the drug. At the six-month follow-up, the drug group was even more likely to recall the experience as deeply mystical and to have integrated the experience into their lives in a positive manner. Presumably it was the interaction of the events of the church service, the prior religiousness of the individual, and the action of the drug on the brain that together created the deep and significant impact of that memorable Good Friday experience.

As with studies of rationality, relationality, and morality, there have been a number of recent brain imaging studies that have sought to observe the activity of the human brain during a religious experience. One study observed changes in brain activity during meditation in both Buddhist

---

[25] Ibid.
[26] Walter N. Pahnke, "Drugs and Mysticism: An Analysis of the Relationship between Psychedelic Drugs and the Mystical Consciousness" doctoral dissertation, Harvard Univeristy, 1963. Also see W. N. Pahnke and W. A. Richards, "Implications of LSD and Experimental Mysticism" (1969), in C. T. Tart, ed., *Altered States of Consciousness* (New York: Wiley, 1990), 399–428.

monks and Catholic nuns.[27] In both groups, the results showed increased frontal lobe activity, and decreased activity in the right parietal lobe (the brain area above and behind the right ear), at the point in time that the person reported reaching a state of total absorption and "oneness." Decreased activity in the right parietal lobe was interpreted as the brain changes associated with absence of a sense of self, often reported in such meditative states (see the diagram on page 34, figure 3.1).

The same investigators also studied brain activity during the ecstatic religious state of speaking in tongues (termed glossolalia). While speaking in tongues, activity in the frontal lobes and left temporal lobe *decreased* significantly. Reduced activity in these brain areas is consistent with the self-report that speaking in tongues involves a loss of intentional control of speaking (frontal lobes providing less intentional control, and the left temporal lobe providing less normal language content). It is important to note that this change in the frontal lobes is opposite to that seen during meditation. Also, in contrast to the reduced right parietal lobe activity seen during meditative states, glossolalia was associated with increased activity in the left parietal area.

Thus, these brain imaging studies suggest that religious states are associated with identifiable changes in the distribution of brain activity. However, these studies also show that religious experiences are not associated with a single brain area or pattern of brain activity, but different religious states are associated with different patterns – in some cases quite opposite patterns of brain activity. Finally, while our religious life and experiences are a manifestation of our brain activity, such states are not inevitably experienced as religious, but they become so within the wider context of our whole personhood – our life memories, beliefs, and social context. Thus, there are a multitude of forms of body and brain activity that can mediate and embody religious experiences and the sense of the presence of God, but any particular brain-body event is experienced as religious or not based the person's expectations and ways of understanding their subjective experiences.

---

[27] A. Newberg et al., (2001) "The Measurement of Regional Cerebral Blood Flow during the Complex Cognitive Task of Meditation: A Preliminary SPECT Study," *Psychiatry Research* 2, (2001):113–122.

BRAIN, BODY, AND HUMAN DISTINCTIVENESS

All of these clinical and experimental observations come together to strongly suggest that the properties that are distinctive of human persons, and that at various times in history have been presumed to be the activity of the soul, are embodied – that is, they are a manifestation of the functioning of our bodies and brains. Given the current state of knowledge in neurology and neuroscience, it is no longer necessary to attribute rationality, relationality, morality, or even religious life to the presence of a nonmaterial soul, simply because we can't imagine how a physical system would do this. Descartes was forced to the conclusion that we must have a nonmaterial soul due to the lack of knowledge during his time of the functioning of the human brain. As far back as 1944, theologian Wolfart Pannenberg offered the following observation, "When the life of the soul is conditioned in every detail by bodily organs and processes, how can it be detached from the body and survive?"[28]

Thus, what is inside us that accounts for our distinctiveness as humankind is not an immaterial thing, such as a soul, that is separate from our bodies and needs a particular form of spiritual care and nurture. Rather, inside us are myriad complex physical functions and processes, shaped both by our physical development and by our history of personal experiences. These functions and processes contribute bits and pieces to who we are as rational, social, moral, and religious whole-physical persons capable of interacting with the physical, social, and spiritual world within which we are embedded.

So, if we are bodies (not bodies with souls), what does it mean to be a person, or to be spiritual? How do physical human beings become persons? How does one become a mature, wise, virtuous, or spiritual person? We take up the challenge of these questions in Part II.

---

[28] Wolfart Pannenberg, *Systematic Theology*, vol. 2 (Grand Rapids, MI: Eerdmans, 1944), 182, as quoted by Joel Green, "What Does It Mean to be Human?" in Malcolm A. Jeeves, *From Cells to Souls – and Beyond* (Grand Rapids, Eerdmans, 2004), 180.

༨

THE FORMATION OF PERSONS:
RETROSPECT AND PROSPECT

REVIEW

In Part I of this book we laid the ground work for a more wholistic, less dualist, understanding of the nature of persons. In Chapter 2, we briefly described the history of the idea that human beings are composed of a body and a soul. We contrasted this body-soul dualism with the alternative proposal that we are bodies with capacities to be soulish, not bodies inhabited by souls. We briefly described the origins of dualism in philosophy, as well as the degree to which this view affected the early church in the form of the Gnostic heresy. This is in contrast to what most modern biblical scholars believe to be a more wholist-monist view of persons in scripture. We also tried to highlight the implications of the modern inclination toward inward and individualist forms of spirituality.

In Chapter 3, we considered some of the evidence from brain science that shows that the soulish capacities of persons are things that our bodies and brains do. There our tactic was to focus on properties of human beings that have at one time or another in Christian history been assigned to the soul: rationality, relationality, morality, and religiousness. In all cases, we found ample evidence that these important human capacities are properties of the functioning of our brains and bodies. Nevertheless, it is rather mind-boggling that such complex, high-level human capacities can emerge from the functioning of neural systems.

PREVIEW

In the three chapters of Part II, we will consider the implications of the embodiment of human nature for the development, formation, and change of persons. In Chapter 4, we consider the relational nature of the mental and social development of children. It is obvious that children mature mentally and socially as the physical structure of their brains form and become mature. But what we will emphasize are the important social influences on the form and direction of mental and social maturation. We describe the formative impact of such interpersonal interactions as imitation, shared attention, attachment, and empathy, as well as language and story.

Chapter 5 takes up the issue of the dynamics of continuing adult personality and character development. Happily for all of us, it is not only children who are open to change and reformation. Adults are also continually changed and transformed – for better or worse – as they experience life. As with children, these formative forces are almost exclusively interpersonal. So, we look again at some of the same processes, but now from the point of view of adult development: imitation, attachments, and life-forming narratives. What is at stake in adult development is the degree to which wisdom and virtue come to characterize persons.

Finally, in Chapter 6, we focus on the processes of change and reformation in the context of those persons for whom prior development and formation have gone awry, often causing them to seek professional help. We rely heavily in this chapter on the processes of personal transformation in psychotherapy, but also describe the power of groups of other persons, such as might be found in the church, in aiding this process of change.

4

꙳

How Bodies Become Persons

GENIE

Genie (a pseudonym) was discovered by Child Protective Services in a home in Los Angeles at the age of thirteen. Since very early childhood, she had been strapped to a potty chair during the day and caged in a crib all night. She was never spoken to and when she was brought food or given minimal other care, she was barked at rather than spoken to. Her father was paranoid and disliked noise, so there were no ambient sounds of conversation, television, or radio to be heard.

When first discovered, Genie was thought to be autistic. She had several rocking and self-stimulating habits and was difficult to engage socially. Because of her limited opportunity for movement (such as walking or playing), her motor development was abnormal. She walked bent over with a type of bunny hop. At first, Genie had no language capacity and was basically mute. With extensive language training, she eventually gained some vocabulary, but she was never able to say words that sounded phonologically entirely correct, and she never developed more than minimal competence in grammar in either her speaking or comprehension of speech. Of course, her social interactions were severely abnormal, with particular problems with anger management and childlike behavioral interactions. It took her several months just to learn how to smile. After several foster placements, she finally ended up in a home for the mentally disabled, where she resides at this writing. As an adult, she lapsed into a state similar to dementia.[1]

---

[1] Susan Curtiss, *Genie: A Psycholinguistic Study of a Modern-Day "Wild Child"* (Boston: Academic Press, 1977).

THE SOCIAL BASIS OF CHILD DEVELOPMENT

Genie was autisticlike, socially inept, linguistically deficient, and generally mentally disabled, but not because of some brain disorder. Rather,
Genie was the victim of severe childhood social deprivation. She had
lived for thirteen years without the usual love of parents, interaction with
other people, and the stimulation gained from exploration of the physical
and cultural world. She is a tragic illustration of the fact that, despite all
the genetic influences that result in normal human bodies and brains, as
well as differences in basic temperament, persons do not come preformed. Rather, at birth we are mentally and socially unformed, amor-
phous, plastic, and open to being shaped by the environment.

Imagine what it must be like to be a newborn. Newborn infants are
assaulted by myriad stimuli – colors, shapes, sounds, textures, and body
sensations. It is all a meaningless confusion. Meaning must be learned,
but learning is not passive. Understanding of a common object, say a
spoon, cannot be gained by merely looking. Children must explore the
spoon with their hands, put it in their mouths, and throw it on the floor
in order to come to understand what it is they are seeing. Understanding
comes about via the feedback from constant interactions with the world.

Infants do have inherent tendencies to interact with other persons.
Fairly soon after birth, the ability to recognize and interact with parents
emerges from this confusion of stimuli. Infants are naturally attuned to pay
attention to faces. Infants prefer to look longer and more intently at faces
than at geometric designs, and they move differently and emit vocaliza-
tions when looking at faces. Babies only a few hours old already engage in
imitative interactions with a parent.[2] Two- to three-day-old babies can
discriminate smiles, frowns, and expressions of surprise and can reliably
recognize the smell of their own mother's breast milk. Newborns can
differentiate their mother's voice from another woman's voice. Thus, fairly
quickly, the dominant stimuli that come to have meaning for infants are
the faces, voices, and physical presence of parents.[3]

---

[2] A. N. Meltzoff and M. K. Moore, "Imitation of Facial and Manual Gestures by Human
     Neonates," *Science* 198 (1977):75–78.
[3] Research described in Daniel Stern, *The Interpersonal World of the Infant: A View from
     Psychoanalysis and Developmental Psychology* (New York: Basic Books, 1985).

Much as a block of marble is not a statue until sculpted, physical human bodies are not complete persons. There is a process of sculpting that all children must undergo in becoming persons. As was clear from the tragic early life of Genie, intelligence, personality, social skills, and character are all products of the sculpting of social experiences. While physical development plays an important role, there are very critical formative processes of interactive social learning that must take place for infants to become persons.[4] From the moment of birth, the most important things to be learned are social!

An important contributor to the formation of children into adults is the unique plasticity in the medium being sculpted – the brain – due to the unprecedented openness of the human nervous system. This openness is most robust during early child development, but remains an important factor throughout life. The only partially preformed, but ever-plastic, infant brain allows developing children to be shaped by social processes known well to developmental psychologists – imitation, shared attention, interpersonal attachment, empathy, and language. This chapter discusses these influences on child development in order to lay a framework for an understanding of the early formation of Christian persons.

THE OPEN AND SELF-ORGANIZING NATURE OF HUMANKIND

How do we become the complex interactive persons that we are? It is increasingly clear to researchers that the fine structure of the brain is formed ("wired") through a kaleidoscope of daily experiences. Genes contribute only a rough blueprint of brain wiring; the rest is formed by a self-organizing process based on continued feedback from action in the world. Thus, the development of intelligence, personality, and character, while influenced to some degree by genes, mostly takes place through complex interactions with the environment.[5] Human beings are neither

---

[4] We use the word "person" to refer to a cognitive and social agent that is more than merely a living body.

[5] An answer to this question is given by Steven Quartz and Terrence Sejnowski in the form of a "neural constructivist manifesto." See Steven Quartz and Terrence Sejnowski, *Liars, Lovers, and Heroes: What the New Brain Science Reveals About How We Become Who We Are* (New York: Quill, 2002), 128.

fixed at birth with certain immutable qualities via genetic endowment, nor are they totally blank slates (*tabula rasa*), to be etched and inscribed by life experiences. Rather, the human mind is a combination of certain predispositions and the experience-based emergence of mental capacities, personality, and character through a continuous history of situational and social interactions. Exploration, give-and-take, and trial and error with the physical and social environment fundamentally change us at the level of our neurons, particularly as children. Within some genetic constraints, the brain is largely a self-organizing system.

This experienced-based, self-organizing nature of human mind and personhood is the result of the very slow physical development that is a relatively unique property of the human brain, particularly the cerebral cortex.[6] Whereas a chimpanzee has an adultlike brain by the end of its second year of life, a similar degree of development is not reached in humans until four to five years later. Remarkably, the frontal lobe (part of the cerebral cortex just behind the forehead) is still maturing in the late teenage years. This brain area is critical for the most sophisticated processes of the mind. Prolonged physical development allows maximal opportunity for brain wiring to be sculpted by the physical, social, and cultural world of the individual. Thus, differences in mental power and sociality between humans and apes are not simply due to differences in the size of the brain, but also to the significantly extended opportunity for social and cultural learning to influence the organization of its fine structure.

The process of self-organization by which the open and dynamic brain and body of an infant becomes an increasingly complex mental system is referred to in modern developmental psychology as *meaning making*.[7] The idea is that the world has no innate meaning to an infant. Therefore, infants must actively engage the world to figure out what it is about. Meaning is found in feedback from action. The actions are, to begin with, quite random, with the possible exception of interactive eye-gaze and facial imitation of the mother. These innate tendencies to orient to faces allow the infant to quickly begin to make social meaning. As children

---

[6]   Quartz and Sejnowski, op. cit., 376.
[7]   E. Tronick and M. Beeghly, "Infants' Meaning-Making and the Development of Mental Health Problems," *American Psychologist* 66, no. 2 (2011):107–119.

become more physically coordinated (that is, having gained some motor meanings), they are increasingly able to explore their world and make more sensory meanings (visual, auditory, touch, kinesthetic). Their mental systems become increasing complex and intelligent by constant sensorimotor interaction with their world. Meaning is made by action, not passively discovered by observation. For example, imagine how much children learn about space when they begin to crawl and move about.

Psychologists have shown that human infants are born with a particular temperament, which by four months can be very broadly characterized as inhibited (20 percent of infants) or bold/fearless (40 percent), with the rest showing a mix of the two styles.[8] However, by four years of age, only 10 percent of children show such extremes in temperament. Thus, the experiences of life during these early years can modify these temperaments. Being born *some* way does not equal forever being *that* way.[9] Even more striking is research where monkeys were bred to be primarily inhibited/fearful or bold in temperament. Later, some of the inhibited/fearful infant monkeys were moved into a cage with uninhibited, nurturing foster mothers. They subsequently became less fearful and less "ramped up" physiologically, as indicated by a reduction in biochemical markers of stress and fear, such as blood levels of the stress hormones adrenaline and cortisol.[10]

The point we wish to emphasize is that intelligence, personality, and character are mostly open programs in the same way that some computer super-games develop new game knowledge as they are played. The program itself gets progressively modified and improved by the experiences of trial-and-success and trial-and-error feedback as the game is played – so also does the developing brain of a child. Thus, our neural openness gives us a great advantage in mental flexibility, allowing our personhood to be shaped for unanticipated roles and challenges.

We now turn to an explanation of some critical processes of child-adult interaction that shape intelligence, personality, and character: imitation, shared attention, emotional attunement, and interpersonal attachments.

[8] Research by Jerome Kagan described in Quartz and Sejnowski, op. cit., 125.
[9] Quartz and Sejnowski, op. cit., 128.
[10] M. Champoux et al., "Serotonin Transporter Gene Polymorphism, Differential Early Rearing, and Behavior in Rhesus Monkey Neonates," *Molecular Psychiatry* 7 (2002):1058–1063.

IMITATION AND CHILD DEVELOPMENT

This openness is not itself entirely sufficient for formation of the person-hood of a child. It needs to be coupled with innate behavioral tendencies to interact with other persons. Infants are born predisposed to imitate other human beings. As early as the first hours of life, it has been shown that an infant will imitate facial gestures, like sticking out the tongue or opening the mouth – and the best part, smiling back. Given the openness of mental systems, the capacity to imitate allows an infant to learn about the nature of other persons. Infants engage in bidirectional learning effects, in which they both learn new behaviors by observing and copying the action of others and learn about the *meaning* of the action of others through their own imitative behavior.[11] Perception and production of behavior (seeing and doing) have a reciprocal influence on one another through the innate capacity to imitate. This perception-action reciprocity lays the foundation for an infant's ability to understand that another person is "like me," with similar behavior and, therefore, similar intentions, thoughts, and feelings.

There is much research to support the notion that acts seen and acts done are coded together in the brain and are therefore tightly linked to one another, providing a basis for "like me" inferences. This idea of similar brain coding for seeing and doing has received considerable support from the discovery of mirror neurons in monkeys (with evidence these neurons are also present in humans). Mirror neurons are found in the motor areas of the cerebral cortex of the brain and are characterized by being similarly active, both while *making* a particular movement oneself and while *observing* the same action being made by another. Observing the actions of others looks, in brain scans, much like perform-ing the act oneself.[12] This mirroring of neural activity becomes a basis for understanding the presumed intention of others, such that observing the

---

[11] Andrew Meltzoff and Jean Decety, "What Imitation Tells Us about Social Cognition: A Rapprochement between Developmental Psychology and Cognitive Neuroscience," *Philosophical Transaction of the Royal Society of London B: Biological Sciences*, 358 (2003):491–500; Andrew Meltzoff, "The 'Like Me' Framework for Recognizing and Becoming an Intentional Agent," *Acta Psychologica*, 124 (2007):26–43.

[12] Research on mirroring the neural activity of the actions, sensations, and emotions of other persons is reviewed by Christian Keysers and Valeria Gazzola, "Towards a Unifying Neural Theory of Social Cognition." in S. Anders et al., eds., *Progress in Brain Research* 156 (2006):379–401.

actions of another person causes one to implicitly imagine doing the same act and, thus, having the same intention to act. Our brains understand the actions of others by simulating what it would be like to do the same action ourselves. While these simulations facilitate our understanding of what another person is doing, they also prime the motor circuits of our own brain in ways that increase the likelihood of imitating the actions we are observing.

This linkage between observed and imitated behavior lays the groundwork for infants to be able to link their first-person experiences of what it is like to behave in a certain way with their observations of other persons. This provides the basis for children to understand the intentions, feelings, and experiences of others. That is, when children observe another person acting in the same way they do when they are expressing a particular intention, or when children see the other person having the same facial expression as they do when they are having a particular feeling or emotion, then they can properly attribute to that other person the same internal intentions or experiences that they had. Thus, this "like me" framework provides infants with the early tools needed to form a mature understanding that others are intentional agents like themselves. This is what is called a *theory of mind*, in that one infers the mental states of other persons based on their behavior, using memories of one's own experiences.

Therefore, for human children to become adults capable of sensitive and nuanced understanding of the social world, they first need to develop the mental capacity to think about the parallels between their own thoughts and actions and those of others. Developmental psychologist Andrew Meltzoff, who studies imitation in infants, makes the following statement about what children need to come to understand in order to develop a theory of mind:

Persons are more than dynamic bags of skin that I can imitate and which imitate me. . . . [P]ersons have internal mental states – such as beliefs, goals and intentions – that predict and explain human action. . . . We are able to recognize that everyone does not share our own desires, emotions, intentions and beliefs. To become a sophisticated mentalizer one needs to analyze both the similarities and differences between one's own states and those of others. That is what makes us human.[13]

---

[13] Ibid., 495 and 498.

Imitation is a mixed blessing. While it facilitates learning about the actions, intentions, and feelings of other persons, it can also put us in conflict with others. The problem is that we not only imitate behavior, we also imitate desire. Perhaps you have observed the following scenario in a room full of young children: A particular toy, say a truck, is being ignored. None of the children are interested in the toy. However, quite randomly, one child will pick up the truck and begin to play with it. Suddenly, that particular truck becomes desired by other children nearby. What a moment earlier was being ignored is now highly desirable. The children are imitating each other's desire as well as their behavior. The problem is that we now have a tug-of-war between two or more children over who gets the toy, eliciting anger and tears. We will explore to a greater extent this process of the imitation of desire later, when we discuss the imitative nature of adult desires.

To summarize, the process of imitation begins very early in infancy and provides one of the important interpersonal dynamics for learning new behaviors. Imitation is a critical process in the development of social behaviors and social knowledge, including a theory of mind. Throughout childhood and adolescence, imitation also plays a role in the development of character and in spiritual formation – a topic we will take up again later.

SHARED ATTENTION

Another relational process that is critical for child social development is shared attention. Shared attention refers to two individuals simultaneously paying attention to the same thing, person, or event. Sharing attention is a fundamental interpersonal process. By six months of age, infants tend to look in the direction that another person turns his or her head, and by one year they will look in the direction of another person's eyes gaze. Children also readily learn to look in the direction where another person is pointing rather than at the finger doing the pointing.

The importance of the very early development of shared attention is that it facilitates learning and development in three important ways. First, attention sharing provides a common set of sensory experiences between a child and an adult for grounding communications and teaching. The common focus of attention provides the topic for what is said. Second, this mechanism is critical in acquiring skills for interpersonal interactions. Relationships between persons always have a topic, and thus children learn to share a topic as they learn to share attention. In infants, the topic may be as simple as an exchange of facial expressions or a bodily interaction, such as tickling. Third, shared attention is reciprocal in ways that engage both persons (parent and child) in a relational system. The child attends to where the parent looks or points, but the parent also shifts the focus of attention to where the child looks or points.

A critical example of the importance of shared attention is its role in language learning. In order for a child to learn what the word "doggie" means, he or she must be able to look at the dog with the parent who is saying the word. Child and parent must share attention to the dog for the child to associate the dog with the spoken word "doggie." Language cannot be learned except through attentions and interactions shared with language-competent adults.

We previously described the critical role of imitation. Imitation presumes some level of shared attention. Behaviors that are imitated are done so in relationship to objects and situations that are the focus of shared attention. The most sophisticated forms of imitation require shared attention in that, for one individual to imitate the behavior of another, there is a need to pay attention to the things the other person is attending to. Therefore, the process of interpersonal imitation is augmented by the sharing of attention, leading to a robust capacity for all sorts of learning and formation of children via their social interactions. Throughout life, all forms of mentoring and instruction will call on the capacity for shared attention to external objects, images, ideas, stories, or memories.

INTERPERSONAL ATTACHMENT

Another important relational process that forms the personality and character of children is the degree and nature of attachments formed with parents. Attachment theory describes an important process of human development that has become increasingly woven into the fabric of thinking about human personality within modern psychology. This theory was introduced in the 1960s by John Bowlby.[14] Attachment theory posited that a primary human motivation is interpersonal relationship – a motive that is at least as important as biological motives such as food and reproduction. Attachment theory hypothesized that relational motivation and behavior was purposeful and necessary for human survival. Babies express attachment-seeking behaviors, such as crying when separated from their primary caregivers, in order to assure proximity with caregivers.

Research has shown that the responses of caregivers to their infants lead to the development in children of one of four attachment styles. *Secure attachment* was found to be a product of fairly consistent parent availability and reliability. Children might protest and become distressed when they were separated from their parents but were happy to see them return and were easily comforted. Bowlby theorized that these children developed an expectation of parental responsiveness. Insecure attachment, however, could take on several different forms. *Preoccupied attachment* was a result of inconsistent parental responsiveness. These children developed behaviors suggesting that they were anxious or uncertain about their parents' reliability. Preoccupied children were never quite sure when the next episode of relational disappointment might occur. *Avoidant attachment* was a more severe form of insecure attachment that was precipitated by even more inconsistent parenting. This parenting was so inconsistent that children developed an expectation of disappointment. When the parents of the avoidant child would finally "show up," the child would often feign disinterest in re-establishing a connection. The most seriously disturbed attachment style was known as *disorganized attachment*. This style was found to be the result of chaotic and abusive parenting (recall the parenting relationships experienced by Genie). This form of attachment, or perhaps nonattachment, often resulted in some form of mental illness. Since these children do not develop an ability to predict parental responsiveness, they end up

---

[14] John Bowlby, *Attachment and Loss:* Vol. 1. *Attachment* (New York: Basic Books, 1969); Vol. 2. *Separation: Anxiety and Anger* (New York: Basic Books, 1973); Vol. 3. *Loss: Sadness and Depression* (New York: Basic Books, 1980).

confused and disorganized in both their pleas for attachment and their responses when attachment is available.

Bowlby theorized, and recent research has substantiated, that these attachment styles have some level of consistency over time. In other words, secure infants tend to grow up to be secure adults, and insecurely attached infants tend to remain insecure as adults. We will revisit the attachment issue in adults in later chapters, but at this point, it is sufficient to state that early infant-caregiver interactions set up a working model of relationships that children carry into adulthood. What we learn about relationships early in life, we use to anticipate what to expect in later relationships. If the responses of our early childhood caregivers were inconsistent, causing development of an anxious attachment style, we will tend, in later life, to be anxious about how our friends or spouse will respond. As a consequence, we may develop unconscious compensatory behaviors with the goal of bringing others into closer proximity. For children, among these behaviors may be tantrums, pouting, cajoling an adult, being silly, and being endearing. In adulthood, grown-up versions of these same behaviors can be readily detected.

We talked earlier about the process of meaning making that is the ongoing task of infants and children as they undergo the process of self-organization. This process is influenced by the security of the child's attachments to caregivers. The more safe and secure a child feels, the more likely the child will explore. And the more exploration a child does, the more meaning is made. This is particularly true for social meaning – that is, what a child comes to understand about the nature of interpersonal relationships. Can persons in the family be trusted? Can strangers be trusted? Human relationships of all kinds are inherently messy and involve lots of mistakes and miscommunications that require ongoing processes of relational error repair. When child and parent have a secure relationship, errors are readily repaired, and greater trust, safety, and security are learned by the child, leading to further tendencies for physical and social exploration.

Recently, psychoanalyst and neuropsychologist Allen Schore recast attachment theory in terms of the neurobiological regulation and dysregulation of emotions, arguing that individuals who have experienced consistently good attachment relationships will have a more resilient neurobiological system for regulating positive and negative emotional states.[15] Schore argues that attachment experiences are processed and stored in the brain as networks of cognitive and emotional memories that continue to shape expectations and behavior in later relationships. Psychiatrist Daniel Siegal has also demonstrated that emotional resilience, mental abilities, and behavioral flexibility are associated with the development of a secure attachment style.[16]

Thus, given the open neural system of children, a critical aspect of their social and psychological development is the nature of interactions with parents and caregivers and the nature of the attachments that form. These attachments create the framework for emotional reactions and social relationships as adults. Furthermore, research has demonstrated that there is intergenerational transmission of attachment styles from parents to children.[17] Mothers with insecure attachment histories who display insecure attachment styles as adults tend to raise insecurely attached babies. In contrast, securely attached mothers tend to raise securely attached infants.

Adolescence is a powerful and often stressful developmental period. Although adolescence is frequently understood as a period when teens are moving away from their parents and becoming more independent, the quality of that autonomy is directly related to the quality of attachment relationships between an adolescent and his or her parents. Adolescents may become less dependent on their parents in practical and social matters, but that doesn't mean parental relationships are unimportant. For adolescents, and even young adults, parents are still critical attachment figures, particularly during times of stress.

While in some ways the attachment behavior of adolescents is not that different from infants, in other ways it is quite different. Adolescents often actively resist relying on their parents. However, this is a natural process that is very much like exploratory behavior in childhood and is facilitated by positive parental attachment. Research suggests that

---

[15]   A. Schore, *Affect Regulation and the Origin of the Self: The Neurobiology of Emotional Development* (Hillsdale, NJ: Lawrance Erlbaum Associates, 1994).

[16]   J. D. Siegal, "An Interpersonal Neurobiology of Psychotherapy: The Developing Mind and the Resolution of Trauma," in M. F. Solomon and D. J. Siegel, eds., *Healing Trauma: Attachment, Mind, Body, and Brain* (New York: W.W. Norton and Co, 2003), 1–56.

[17]   See research cited in David J. Wallin, *Attachment in Psychotherapy* (New York: Guildford, 2007), 23–24, 31–34.

adolescent autonomy-seeking behavior is highly correlated with positive parental relationships. They are free to explore, because they know that their parents remain available if needed. And, of course, this exploratory opportunity makes possible the development of peer and romantic relationships.[18]

EMPATHY

The relational processes we have described thus far – imitation, shared attention, and attachment – all come together to foster in children a sense of empathy for the feelings of other persons. The primitive precursor of empathy, in the emotional attunement between mother and child, is an innate process – when mother cries, baby cries; when mother smiles, baby smiles. Infants have the tendency to attune their emotions to those of others around them and, thus, to have a basis for understanding what other persons are feeling. Of course, this attunement is bidirectional – parents experience the emotions of the child, as the child experiences parents' emotions.

Children learn empathy by being shown empathy. When a child first takes a fall, he or she is flooded with physical sensations; it takes an attuned parent or caregiver who says, "That hurts doesn't it?" for the child to understand and label the emotional experience that accompanies the physical sensation. Over time, this emotional attunement on the part of the parent will allow the child to display the same empathy toward their parents. Mother may bang her knee against a coffee table and the child will spontaneously say, "Ouch! That hurts mommy . . . me sorry!" This reciprocal attunement contributes to the development of what we described earlier as a Theory of Mind – the ability of children to recognize that another individual (the parent) has a separate mind, but with feelings, thoughts, and perspectives similar to their own. They learn that others sometimes share their thoughts and feelings, and sometimes they do not.

[18] Joseph P. Allen and Deborah Land, "Attachment in Adolescence," in J. Cassidy and P. R. Shaver, eds., *Handbook of Attachment: Theory, Research, and Clinical Implications* (New York: Guilford Press, 1999), 319–335.

Clearly, the developmental achievements of empathy and a Theory of Mind require imitation and shared attention. These capacities are also enhanced through good, secure attachment, and are disrupted by poor attachment. Anxiously attached individuals have a harder time separating their perspectives and feelings from those of other persons. They seem to assume that if they are feeling or thinking something, then others around them must be feeling or thinking the same things. Disorganized attached individuals may even have a hard time separating self from others, with fuzzy personal and physical boundaries. It may be hard for them to recognize where they stop and another person begins.

LANGUAGE AND STORIES

Sometime during the second year of life, language learning kicks into high gear and accelerates exponentially. It is obvious, but worth noting, that language is impossible for children to learn outside of a rich and constant verbal interchange with parents and other persons. Thus, this mastery of language is another relational process that does much to form the intelligence, personality, and character of children.

The capacity for language rests upon a particular architecture within the brain that is relatively unique to human beings and present in some form at birth. The existence of a genetic blue print for language has been suggested in studies using brain scans. Functional magnetic resonance imaging (fMRI) makes visible those areas of the brain that are particularly active during various kinds of thinking and experiencing. Using fMRI, activity has been shown to occur in specific areas in the cerebral cortex of the brain when people are listening to speech. This activity is also seen in year-old infants who have not yet learned to speak or understand speech.

However, even this genetically predisposed language system is highly malleable and plastic, requiring social experience to become functional. Brain systems involved in language develop specific "wiring" based upon experience with language. For example, research has shown that infants start life with the ability to tell the difference between all human language sounds. They are alerted when a repeating vowel changes from "la" to "ra." However, within a few years of hearing their native language, they progressively lose the ability to detect differences between sounds that do not occur in their native tongue.[19] If the tongue they are learning does not include this distinction, they soon are no longer able to "hear" the difference. In fact, if language is not used at all, due to some form of social or sensory deprivation, the language capacity can suffer permanent damage and loss of function, such as Genie's syntactically and phonetically abnormal speech.[20]

The dependence of language development on being embedded in a rich social and linguistic environment is illustrated in attempts to teach language to chimpanzees. It is clear that gorillas and chimpanzees in the wild do not have a true language, although they certainly communicate with vocal and gestural codes. Nevertheless, research since the 1960s has suggested that minimal language like abilities can be developed in apes when given intensive training in a laboratory. However, a chimpanzee named Kanzi is remarkable with respect to the acquisition of language by a non-human primate.[21] Kanzi developed an English comprehension vocabulary that includes more than 500 words, which is roughly equivalent to that of a two-and-a-half-year-old child. This case turns out to have been particularly outstanding primarily because of two factors that were not typical of previous attempts to teach language to a chimpanzee. First, Kanzi was exposed to a language system right from birth because he was present while his mother was attempting to learn the token language in the laboratory. Second, from birth Kanzi was also consistently immersed in a rich human language environment, via interactions with human caretakers and experimenters, even though they were mostly attending to his mother. The moral of the Kanzi story is that, like human children, whatever language capacity a chimpanzee can master is dependent upon early developmental exposure to a richly linguistic social environment.

Biological anthropologist Terrence Deacon provides an important analysis of what learning a language contributes to the development of human thought and behavior.[22] As the capacity for language emerges in

[19] P. K. Kuhl et al., "Linguistic Experience Alters Phonetic Perception in Infants by 6 Months of Age," *Science*, 31 (1992):606–608.

[20] Susan Curtiss, op. cit.

[21] Sue Savage-Rumbaugh and Roger Lewin, *Kanzi: The Ape at the Brink of the Human Mind* (New York: Wiley, 1994).

[22] Terrance Deacon, *The Symbolic Species: The Co-evolution of Language and the Brain* (New York: W. W. Norton & Co., 1997).

children, it provides important advantages to mental capacities and social behaviors. First, language *distances us from the demands of immediate motivations and needs.* That is, language facilitates postponing gratification of immediate needs by the ability to consider alternative actions using language-dependent thoughts about the future – often referred to as "what if" scenarios. Second, via language we *form a self-concept.* Language allows us to have thoughts or express sentences that include the idea of "me." It thus facilitates self-reflection and self-understanding. Third, language provides the basis for *expanded empathy.* Once children become sufficiently competent at understanding language, they learn a great deal about the lives and experiences of other people through these stories. Fourth, language facilitates a *common mind among groups of people.* Common semantics, metaphors, and stories create families and cultural groups with similar world views. Stories of the past, ongoing conversations about present events, and the shared concepts signaled by words are the glue that holds local groups and cultures together. Children are brought into the worldview of their parents, family, and eventually wider social groups via language. Finally, *ethical behavior* is enhanced by language, because it holds and communicates the values of communities in terms of statements about what is good and and what is bad.

Thus, language opens the malleable minds of children to a world of new complex ideas about the physical and social world. It also allows them to know vicariously the experiences of others. Telling children fanciful imaginative tales or reading stories to them (often at bedtime) are wonderful ways to entertain and relate to children. But such story-telling is also an important way of illustrating and teaching values and virtues that contribute to the development of their characters. Story narrative allows children to imagine new situations, vicariously try out a range of new behaviors, and safely experience the positive or negative consequences, forming rich impressions in their minds about what is good and bad, right and wrong, and conducive or not to the well-being of others.

For example, Aesop's fables are stories that children love, but they also include important teaching about persistence ("The Hare and the Tortoise"), being fooled by appearances ("A Wolf in Sheep's Clothing"), the tendency to degrade what one cannot possess ("The

Fox and the Grapes"), the problem of being dishonest ("The Boy who Cried Wolf"), and the potential future benefits of helping someone in need ("The Lion and the Mouse"). These stories are so deeply embedded in our cultural unconscious that the whole story scenario and its implications can be brought to mind by a simple term, such as "sour grapes" or "crying wolf." Thus, these stories have helped form our view of the social world and how to successfully live within it.

The importance of stories in understanding the world and managing our lives is powerfully expressed by philosopher Alisdair MacIntyre.

It is through hearing stories about wicked stepmothers, lost children, good but misguided kings, wolves that suckle twin boys, youngest sons who receive no inheritance but must make their own way in the world and eldest sons who waste their inheritance on riotous living and go into exile to live with the swine, that children learn or mis-learn both what a child and what a parent is, what the cast of characters may be in the drama into which they have been born and what the ways of the world are. Deprive children of stories and you leave them unscripted, anxious stutterers in their actions as in their words.[23]

WHEN DEVELOPMENT GOES AWRY

As we have seen, the quality and quantity of interactions between children and parents or other adults, as well as other children, is critical for their mental and social development. Tragically, there are children who are born with brain disorders that disrupt this process. Autism is a prime example. Children with autism are characterized by a marked disruption in their capacities for social interaction and communication. They become focused on certain objects and/or repetitive behaviors, rather than on people and social interactions. They tend not to respond to pointing, or to use pointing to share attention with caregivers. They have poor eye contact and are less responsive to their own name than nonautistic children. In most cases, their language development is significantly impaired. All of the formative processes we have discussed – imitation, shared attention, attachment, empathy, and language – are

---

[23] Alasdair MacIntyre, *After Virtue: A Study in Moral Theology*, 3rd ed. (Notre Dame, IN: University of Notre Dame Press, 2007), 216.

disturbed in these children. Thus, due to their reduced ability to interact with others, particularly with their parents, children with autism suffer significant limitations in their mental and social formation.

The dependence of normal development on social interaction is also tragically highlighted in cases where otherwise normal children received adequate food and shelter, but were deprived for many years of necessary human contact, interaction, and love. We began this chapter with the story of Genie, a remarkable illustration of the severe effects on children who are deprived of human interaction and love. As an infant, Genie was neither mentally retarded nor autistic. However, thirteen years of persistent social neglect resulted in her exhibiting symptoms of those conditions. What seems to be so natural and inherent in child development turns out to be deeply dependent on continuous physical, emotional, and social interactions with parents, family, and the broader social world.

Unfortunately, Genie is not the only child who has suffered from such social neglect. Revelation of the condition of children living in Romanian orphanages after the demise of dictator Nicolae Ceausescu was shocking. Under Ceausescu's economic and social policies, thousands of Romanian parents had no choice but to leave their children to be raised in state-run orphanages. The mass housing and feeding in these institutions was markedly devoid of human contact, care, and love. While basic physical care was provided, any other form of human physical or verbal inter-action was minimal. The outcome for these children was retarded phys-ical, mental, and social development.

Much like Genie, some of these orphaned children developed symp-toms like those of autism although they were not autistic. They would sit in dirty cribs and rock themselves endlessly. As children grew older, they were housed – almost caged – in large groups where interactions among the children were barbaric, with older children bullying younger children and everyone abusing the most weak or sickly. Researchers found that the majority of these children grew up with over responsive stress hormone systems, and the longer they lived in the deprived conditions, the higher their stress hormone levels were.[24] In addition, the mental

---

[24]   M. R. Gunnar et al., "Salivary Cortisol Levels in Children Adopted from Romanian Orphanages," *Development and Psychopathology* 13, no. 3 (2001):611–628.

development of these orphans was impaired.[25] Interestingly, recent research has shown that if these children were placed into the homes of loving foster families within the first two years of life, the negative impact of these dire conditions on their mental development was substantially reduced.

FORMATION OF PERSONS

This chapter has outlined some of the interpersonal forces that come together to form infants into adult persons. We are born bodies with needs and developing sensory, motor, and mental systems that are very plastic and subject to formation based on our experiences. In the process of growing up, infants imitate others (particularly their parents), share attention with others, form emotional attachments, learn empathy for the experiences and feelings of others, develop the ability to share thoughts and feelings through language, and hear stories that provide vicarious experiences. All of these processes strongly influence the personality and character of the persons they are becoming. None of these processes happen without human interaction.

It is the premise of this book that, if we are indeed embodied persons and not souls or spirits inhabiting bodies, then these processes of child development and formation are important to consider also from the standpoint of Christian formation, as it is fostered within the life of Christian groups (families, circles of friends, communities of Christians, and the church). The formation of the personhood of children is inherently social and emerges through interactions with others. However, it is not that children are *passively* determined by their environment, but, rather, their interactions with the physical and social environment as active agents provide them with the necessary feedback for learning and development.

Clearly, the embodiment of the personhood of children has been implicitly recognized by the church in its programs for children. The role of physical (brain) development and the necessity of social

---

[25] C. A. Nelson III et al., "Cognitive Recovery in Socially Deprived Young Children: The Bucharest Early Intervention Project," *Science* 318, no. 5858 (December 2007):1937–1940.

interaction and communication are almost universally built into church curricula for children. For some reason, our dualist presuppositions about persons create a disconnection between our understanding of Christian formation in children and our comprehension of the forces at work in adult Christian life. It is not true that the impact on human development of all of these processes of ongoing reciprocal interaction with one's social environment comes to an end somewhere in later childhood or early adolescence. Rather, this developmental process is *ongoing*, allowing for continuing development, formation, and change as adults. It is to this continuing process of adult formation that we turn in the next chapter.

5

⁓

How Relationships Shape Us

Meanwhile Saul was still breathing out murderous threats against the Lord's disciples. He went to the high priest and asked him for letters to the synagogues in Damascus, so that if he found any there who belonged to the Way, whether men or women, he might take them as prisoners to Jerusalem. As he neared Damascus on his journey, suddenly a light from heaven flashed around him. He fell to the ground and heard a voice say to him, "Saul, Saul, why do you persecute me?"

"Who are you, Lord?" Saul asked.

"I am Jesus, whom you are persecuting," he replied. "Now get up and go into the city, and you will be told what you must do."

Saul spent several days with the disciples in Damascus. At once he began to preach in the synagogues that Jesus is the Son of God. All those who heard him were astonished and asked, "Isn't he the man who raised havoc in Jerusalem among those who call on this name? And hasn't he come here to take them as prisoners to the chief priests?" Yet Saul grew more and more powerful and baffled the Jews living in Damascus by proving that Jesus is the Messiah. [Acts 9:1–6; 19–22 NIV]

RE-FORMING PERSONS

We are often caused to wonder whether adults can change. Can you teach an old dog new tricks? It is obvious that children change readily. They are adaptable and very open to new learning. The processes involved in the formation of children, and the most significant influences on their development, were the topic of the last chapter. In this chapter, we consider similar processes of change in adults that allow for their continued formation and re-formation.

Although most Christian conversions are not as dramatic as Paul's experience on the Damascus road, nevertheless there are stories in most Christian communities of dramatic and relatively sudden conversions, after which the person is notably different in many ways. In some way, God was revealed, the gospel was comprehended, and the person was changed. However, most adult formation and change is more progressive and more difficult to discern on a day-to-day basis. Significant change takes months, years, or even decades. Even relatively sudden conversions are not totally out of the blue, but are the culmination of a period of more subtle, subliminal change and formation in the individual. What is more, a critical single conversion event must be followed by months and years of progressive incorporation of the implication of the conversion into the personhood of the convert. Such was certainly the case with Paul.

This chapter on adult development and change is not so much about sudden conversions as about the various influences and causes of the progressive changes that adults can, and typically do, undergo. Two important perspectives carry over from the previous chapter: (1) the same processes that form children are also influential in adults, albeit in somewhat different forms, and (2) the influences that produce the most significant change are outcomes of our social embeddedness.

Before venturing into thoughts about adult formation, two additional points are worth making regarding relationships and social embeddedness. First, while relationships with others are something we *do*, it is also true that relationships are what we *are*. We are what our history of relationships has built into us. We need social relationships like the body needs oxygen, but also like stone needs a sculptor to become a work of art (good or bad). We cannot become healthy adult persons without relationships. To flourish and to mature into persons of wisdom and Christian virtue, we need the shaping that comes with the best sorts of human relationships. Unfortunately, it is also true that inadequate or dysfunctional interpersonal relationships and interactions can create persons who are not mature and have difficulty flourishing.

Second, we must always be clear that the terms *interact* and *relate*, which we will use often, denote a two-way street. We must not understand these as processes done to us as passive elements (like how a block of marble is shaped by a sculptor, despite our previous use of that metaphor). Rather, we always play an active role in relationships. Whatever we become or are becoming is a matter of both us and others – our actions and others' responses, and our responses to others' actions.

THE MATURATION OF SELF-ORGANIZING SYSTEMS

In describing the development of children in the previous chapter, we made the point that the human nervous system is an open program. That is, the preprogramming of genes has only a very general influence on the processes that create the sort of person we become. Openness to experience allows for great flexibility in our formation, particularly the formation of our most human characteristics: intelligence, personality, character, and the assimilation of cultural modes of thought and behavior.

This quality of openness to being shaped and formed by experiences does not end in childhood, but extends across the lifespan, at least to some degree. And there is proof: Compared with fifty-year-olds, the treelike branches of the nerve cells (dendrites) in the memory systems of healthy eighty-year-olds have been found to be 35 percent *more* complex.[1] This suggests that there is sufficient openness continuing throughout life for adult experiences and social relationships to reform us when necessary. New experiences or changes in life circumstances can enhance knowledge and skills, and also alter character and personality. Even in old age, mental capacities can be maintained and enhanced by mental stimulation, novelty, a positive self-concept, exercise, and a rich family and social context.

The reality of changes in the adult brain is illustrated in a study of the brains of London taxi drivers. Since London streets are not laid out in a grid but are a complex maze of streets running every which way, including many one-way streets, driving a taxi makes constant demands on spatial memory. It has been found that the brain areas involved in spatial

---

[1]   S. J. Buell and P. D. Coleman, "Quantitative Evidence for Selective Dendritic Growth in Normal Human Aging but Not in Senile Dementia," *Brain Research* 214 (1981):23–41.

memory get progressively larger the longer a person works as a taxi driver in London.[2] It is our contention that the continued openness and plasticity of human mental systems is also critically important in considering the nature of Christian formation and growth among adults.

A theory borrowed from applied mathematics, called the *theory of complex dynamical systems*, has advanced our understanding of formation and change in very complex, open, and self-organizing systems such as biological organisms, human societies, and economies. This is a technical theory about how really complex characteristics (like minds and person-alities) can emerge from myriad ongoing interactions between the millions of parts (like neurons) making up a system (like an organism or person). This theory is also about adaptability and change.

An ant colony is a helpful example that is often used to illustrate a dynamical system. Consider each ant as one of the many parts, and the colony as the whole system. Because of the constant, ongoing interac-tions among all of the individual ants, the colony comes to function as a whole unified system. Because it is a system rather than a loose assem-blage of individual ants, the colony interacts with its surrounding envi-ronment as a single organism. The colony comes to have whole-system characteristics that cannot be attributed to the characteristics of individ-ual ants (just as human beings have characteristics as persons that cannot be attributed to individual brain cells). Colonies do things, such as building and maintaining nests or going on mass foraging expeditions, that are not due to the plans or decisions of any individual ant. The action of the colony emerges, not just from something about individual ants, but from the interactive patterns that come to characterize the colony, based on a massive quantity of small physical and chemical interactions across tens of thousands of individual ants.

Everything we have already said about the self-forming nature of the human mind and person during child development is what one would expect if the human brain and body were such a dynamic system – that is, a colony of neurons instead of ants. Humans are both *dynamic* in the common sense of the word and *dynamical* in this technical sense. There

[2] E. A. Maguire, K. Woollett, and H. J. Spiers, "London Taxi Drivers and Bus Drivers: A Structural MRI and Neuropsychological Analysis," *Hippocampus* 16, no. 12 (2006):1091–1101.

are characteristics of us (like thinking, deciding, expressing emotions, and having inner experiences) that are not due to any particular neuron. Rather, these important characteristics depend on the patterns that come to exist across myriad interactions among hundreds of millions of neurons.

What is most important to our current discussion about the formation of persons is that the characteristics of such systems can help us understand the nature of human formation and change. One important characteristic of dynamical systems is that they always retain the potential to reorganize in ways that result in new system characteristics. This happens whenever the system is destabilized by an inability to successfully interact with its surroundings. To continue the analogy of an ant colony, a change in the nature of the local food supply can cause the colony to adapt and learn (literally "learn" as a system) new strategies for finding and gathering food. The characteristics of the colony change in ways that meet the new challenge. Interestingly, newer (younger) dynamical systems (including ant colonies or human bodies) reorganize readily, but older systems, although they are still capable of reorganization, are more robust and less likely to change significantly, except in the case of a major destabilization.

We human beings are also complex dynamical systems (very much more complex than an ant colony) that organize and reorganize in the process of interacting with our surroundings, both physical and social. We continually adapt and incorporate new system characteristics through our ongoing life experiences. As we get older, the reorganizations are generally less remarkable than those that occurred when we were younger.

Situations that force reorganization are called, in the parlance of dynamical systems theory, "catastrophes" – a technical word that merely refers to a significant mismatch between a system and its surroundings. For example, ant colonies have been shown to change their behavior when important changes occur in their environment, such as changes in the availability of certain foods – a catastrophe from the point of view of the colony as an organized system. Catastrophes in the lives of persons (for example, coping with a change in the demands of one's job or with a new co-worker) can force reorganization of the person in major or minor ways, depending on what is demanded by the challenges of the new situation.

Saul, on the road to Damascus, encountered not only a remarkable event, but also a rather dramatic catastrophe in his person. His previous understanding of God and his Judaic faith, as well as his conceptions of Jesus and his followers, were forced to undergo a significant reformation. His previous beliefs, ideas, values, and emotional commitments no longer fit the new realities he was encountering. The blinding light out of which God spoke was paralleled in impact by the destabilization and disequilibrium created by the mismatch between what he knew and believed – his previous pattern of self-organization – and the new information he was encountering.

Despite a dramatic catastrophe and subsequent major changes in his life, there was still much of the previous Saul present and recognizable in the reorganized Paul. He was largely the same highly effective and committed person. His friends would still have recognized his personality as his. He would still have all of the same memories. He still had the benefit of his superior Hebrew and Greek education. However, all of this had been reformed around a new core. Now there were new (and progressively reforming) interrelationships among all of his previous ideas, memories, experiences, and emotions.

Similarly, despite the many changes, small and large, that we all undergo throughout our lives, we remain recognizably ourselves. Our friends are not shocked to find us today an entirely different personality than the person they encountered yesterday. This is the case because systems that are forced to reorganize preserve as much of the prior forms of organization as possible. The current system is a more complex *variant* of the old system, only now able to meet new circumstances in the surrounding world.

To summarize, the very nature of the kind of complex physical systems that constitute us as human beings means that we are continually open to change and reformation, even as adults. Changes are prompted by catastrophes, in which our current self is no longer able to deal adequately with our circumstances. The younger the person, the more likely are personal reorganizations, but older systems still change. Changes that take place generally preserve most of the characteristics of the previous state, allowing for growth but with the continued preservation of the integrity of ourselves as particular persons.

ATTACHMENT AND OPENNESS TO CHANGE

Forms of interpersonal attachment that develop in childhood continue to be relevant to adult formation and change. Secure versus insecure forms of attachment influence the likelihood we will explore new situations, meet new friends, or entertain new ideas. Less secure attachment generally means a more rigid system that is less open to change and reorganization in the face of catastrophe. Out of fear, change is resisted. Or, if change occurs, less secure persons tend to change in ways that protect and preserve too much of the previous system (the previous psychological framework). Persons who have more secure attachment styles are characterized by nondefensive openness to the inherent messiness of new situations and relationships. Therefore, they seek out new social situations and meet them with greater flexibility, and thus the outcome of change is more likely to be truly adaptive and productive of personal growth.

Consider a simple example of a young woman who grew up in a family where males were treated as more valuable than females. When she would attempt to speak up in the family, she would be ignored or even told not to interrupt. As an adult she became a competent lawyer, but continually found herself submitting to men, even when they were her peers. She did this despite the fact that her co-workers gave her feedback that she did not appropriately assert herself, especially in situations where she was the expert or the higher ranking attorney. Her insecurity, reflective of her family history, made it difficult for her to incorporate the feedback of her peers and to change in ways that allowed her to become more comfortable in asserting herself. Based on insecurity from the past, she faced these situations by defending her current self and resisting change and growth.

Most of us acknowledge the truth of such influences of our early life experiences, but we don't like it! We cling to ideas of complete free will and individual autonomy, making it hard to admit that these early interactions have such a strong impact on us. But, given the habits and propensities assembled in our early lives, we tend to approach interpersonal problems in characteristic ways, some of which are unhealthy and limit openness and personal growth. When we have interpersonal problems, one defensive maneuver is to attribute the problem to the other person, rather than taking responsibility ourselves. Alternatively, if our early relational history has trained us to feel overly responsible for everything, we continually blame ourselves for everything. Another common response is to embrace the predominant message of popular therapeutic culture that, "though this problem is mine, I am a victim of my upbringing and am not responsible for what has happened to me." Thus, we presume that we have very little control over ourselves in interpersonal situations. Alternatively, a history of more secure relationships with others allows us to escape the tendency to blame others, ourselves, or our developmental history. Mostly importantly, security allows us to be nondefensive and open in facing new life challenges and new interpersonal relationships.

Nevertheless, if we are complex dynamical systems, there is always the possibility of reorganization of ourselves and growth as persons, based on new experiences. New secure and safe relationships are important to open us up to embrace the messiness of new experiences and develop new sorts of relationships with other persons. However, in the face of a significant prior history of bad relationships and insecure attachments, it may take some time spent within a different sort of relationship, such as a supportive friend, spouse, or perhaps therapist, to become open to change. When such a person can form new and healthier relationships and attachments, growth becomes possible. For example, research is suggesting that individuals with insecure attachment styles can develop secure attachment styles through new relationships (such as in therapy, marriage or friendship).[3] To become open and adaptable persons, we need other persons to whom we are healthily attached and with whom we can mutually foster openness and growth. In the end, what we all need is the sort of interdependence based on love, friendship, and collegiality that enhances and encourages continued development and maturity.

UNCONSCIOUSNESS IMITATION

In the last chapter, we discussed the critical role of imitation (particularly of parents) in the development of children. But imitation is not something done only by children. It is a process that goes on continually even

---

[3]   David J. Wallin. *Attachment in Psychotherapy* (New York: Guilford Press, 2007).

in adults. However, since imitation happens unconsciously, we do not notice. Nevertheless, what we imitate in others readily becomes part of our own behavior repertoire, shaping what we do and ultimately what sort of person we become.

There are many simple, everyday demonstrations of the effects we have on one another through imitation. For example, if someone stands in the middle of a sidewalk and looks up at the sky, most everyone who walks by also looks up at the sky. Someone in a group yawns, and others tend to do the same. At the beginning of a song in church, if one person stands, everybody stands. The contagious behavior of large crowds is based on our strong tendency to imitate one another, amplified as the crowd begins to act in unison, be it in positive or negative ways.

A great many research studies illustrate rather dramatically the contagious nature of behavior through imitation. For example, investigators have described what they call the chameleon effect, which refers to our imitation of the postures, mannerisms, and facial expressions of the people around us.[4] We unconsciously and unintentionally change our actions to match those of the people we are around. In most cases, the influence goes directly from what we see to what we do without conscious deliberation. For this reason, the imitative process is referred to in psychology as the "perception-behavior expressway ... the mere perception of another's behavior automatically increases the likelihood of engaging in that behavior oneself."[5]

Although we might admit a tendency to imitate another person's *behavior*, we nevertheless presume that at least our *desires* – as well as our motives, goals, and attitudes – are autonomous and independent of influence from other persons. However, research shows that these more complex and pervasive aspects of our personhood are also influenced by imitation of others outside of our awareness. For example, research has shown that our attitudes can be unconsciously primed by the attitudes we observe in others, making related behaviors more likely to occur. One

[4] T. L. Chartrand and J. A. Bargh, "The Chameleon Effect: The Perception-Behavior Link and Social Interaction," *Journal of Personality and Social Psychology* 76, no. 6 (1999):893–910.

[5] A. Dijksterhuis and J. A. Bargh, "The Perception-Behavior Expressway: Automatic Effects of Social Perception on Social Behavior," in M. P. Zanna, ed., *Advances in Experimental Social Psychology* 33 (San Diego: Academic Press, 2001), 1–40.

study showed that exposure to a person acting rudely in one context increases the likelihood that we will act rudely in an immediately follow-ing (but separate) social context. Many similar studies have shown the effects of this sort of implicit imitation on both complex goal-associated behaviors (for example, performing better or worse on an intelligence test) and interpersonal attitudes (for example, competitiveness versus cooperativeness).[6]

Thus, we can see that our tendency to imitate one another is both good news and bad news. One of the important ways our behavior changes, immediately and in the long-term, is by having new and different models to imitate. If those around us are caring, mature, wise, and virtuous, then our behavior tends to become similar as we imitate them. However, if those around us are rude, immature, unwise, and lacking in virtue, then we will tend to act accordingly. Whether we notice it or not, we are constantly influencing and being influenced by each other's behaviors, attitudes, desires, and goals through *reciprocal imitation*.

The impact of imitation is not limited to actions and desires, but, in addition, *actions influence thought*.[7] What we are doing with our bodies has a profound influence on what we are thinking and how we are thinking about it. Programming of action by the brain is integrated with all other mental processes, and sensing our own movement feeds back to further reinforce and modulate what we think and feel. For example, research has shown that telling children to gesture while attempting to comprehend instructions regarding a mental task makes it more likely that they will profit from the instructions and allows them

---

[6] Studies showing the role of imitation on many different behaviors include the follow-ing: walking slower or behaving rudely (J. A. Bargh, M. Chen, and L. Burrows, "Automaticity of Social Behavior: Direct Effects of Trait Construct and Stereotype-activation on Action," *Journal of Personality and Social Psychology* 71, no. 2 (1996):230–244); performing better or worse on an intelligence test (A. Dijksterhuis and A. van Knippenberg, "The Relation between Perception and Behavior, or How to Win a Game of Trivial Pursuit," *Journal of Personality and Social Psychology* 74, no. 4 (1998):865–877); and competitiveness versus coopera-tiveness (J. A. Bargh et al., "The Automated Will: Nonconscious Activation and Pursuit of Behavioral Goals," *Journal of Personality and Social Psychology* 81, no. 6 (2001):1014–1027).

[7] Susan Goldin-Meadow and Sian L. Beilock, "Action's Influence on Thought: The Case of Gesture," *Perspectives on Psychological Science* 5, no. 6 (2010):664–674.

to perform the subsequent task more accurately.[8] Thus, much like these gestures, behaviors that we imitate have a deep influence on the way we think, and these mental processes have an impact of what we do in the future.

The process of imitation – of both behavior and desire – stands at the core of modern television advertising. No longer do advertisements tout the merits of the product; rather, they show attractive people happily in possession of and using the product. We desire the product and tend to buy it, not based on its merit, but based on our imitation of the people we see in the commercial. The American Dream is not something inherent in the world or in the innate desires of all human beings. Rather, it is a complex of desires acquired through the process of imitation of those around us and constantly reformed and infinitely expanded through the processes of advertising.

This process of forming desires, based on observation of those around us, stands at the core of the Mimetic Theory (that is, imitation theory) proposed by French literary critic René Girard. The power of imitation will make it highly likely that two persons in close proximity will come to desire the same thing: He sees her new car and desires to have such a car himself. However, as Girard points out, desire for the same object leads almost inevitably to competition and rivalry. Remember our example in the previous chapter about children in a nursery and an ignored and unwanted toy. Should one child come to show interest in the toy (pick it up and start to play with it), the interest of other children nearby is immediately piqued, and they grab for the formerly ignored and unwanted toy. What results is a tug-of-war and escalating interchild rivalry.

So it is also with adults, although the expressions of rivalry are more subtle. Margaret hadn't even considered being an assistant manager in her company until her co-worker started talking about it, but now they are competitors for the job. Roger wasn't very interested in being a good golfer until he started golfing with his buddies. Now he is out to beat his friends, and the rivalry is getting increasingly intense. When browsing through clothes in the teen department, Sarah wasn't finding much of

---

[8] S. Ehrich, S. C. Levin, and S. Goldin-Meadows, "The Importance of Gesture in Children's Spatial Reasoning," *Developmental Psychology* 42 (2006):1259–1268.

interest until she saw another teen pick up and consider a particular sweater. Now she wants to buy that same sweater. Unfortunately, the problem of rivalry has a way of escalating, because we also tend to imitate each other's competitive behaviors and attitudes. Soon the original object of the rivalry is forgotten, and the rivalry itself takes center stage. Finding ways of avoiding and escaping the sorts of imitative desire that spawns acquisitiveness and rivalry is an important issue to be considered in rethinking the nature of Christian formation.

Personal formation is a deeply social and interpersonal process. We are social creatures who are significantly interdependent and not as autonomous in our behaviors, goals, and desires as we typically imagine. We absorb ways of acting, thinking, and valuing from one another through imitation. Thus, the process of personal growth toward becoming persons of wisdom and virtue is strongly influenced by the nature of the communities in which we participate. We form each other through reciprocal imitation.

STORIES WE LIVE BY

In the previous chapter, we saw how reading stories and telling fanciful imaginative tales to children is an important way of imparting values, behaviors, and worldviews that contribute to the development of their characters. Story narrative allows children to imagine new situations, vicariously try out various behaviors and safely experience the consequences, forming rich impressions in their minds about what is good and bad, right and wrong, and conducive of well-being. But stories continue to form and reform adults. As we tell each other stories about our own experiences or the exploits of others, read novels, or watch movies or TV shows, we are continually (albeit subtly) shaped. Through these stories, we gain new perspectives on life situations, new possibilities for behavior, and new character models for imitation. While the personality and character of adults is not as plastic and malleable as those of children, they nevertheless are still sufficiently open to be influenced by stories, novels, movies, parables, and the like.

The power of stories lies in the brain's capacity to imaginatively simulate the behaviors being narrated. The process of understanding the actions of persons in a story requires that the systems of our brain that control our own behavior become engaged in a process of internally simulating the actions that constitute the story. We understand the narrative by imaging what it would be like if we were doing what the hero, villain, or victim in the story is described as doing. We do not passively comprehend stories, but mentally engage in simulations of the action. The result is not a memory of the mere abstract details of the story, but rather a behavioral residue from comprehending the story using the neural processes by which we organize our own actions.

In the processes of human relationships, we inevitably communicate to one another implicit and explicit stories that we assimilate into our perspectives and behavioral tendencies. The stories we tell one another, combined with our own narrative appreciation of the events of our own lives, provide a fundamental basis of our comprehension of the meaning of events, the lives and experiences of other persons, and the nature of ourselves as persons. Thus, narratives shape who we are and how we understand ourselves in the world.

In psychology, the power of story is captured in the idea of scripts. This is a metaphor, borrowed from the theater, implying that we live out situations in our lives according to roughly defined scripts. We carry these scripts around in unconscious memories that guide us through different situations. A very simple example is a restaurant script. We know implicitly the basic pattern for the sequence of events that typically happen when eating in a restaurant (being seated at a table, reading a menu, ordering, waiting for food to be brought, and so forth), including what we should and should not do and what we expect others to do and not do. We enter a restaurant experience expecting to play our role in this script.

Scripts cover all sorts of areas of our lives, including work, play, church, and, most importantly, our relationships with parents, spouses, children, and friends. Even more deeply, we all have in our minds the rough outline of a life script (potential life story) that creates our expectations and guides our decisions regarding large issues such as school, marriage, work, recreation, and religiousness. The fact that children tend to lead lives similar to the lives of their parents is because life scripts are strongly influenced by what children grow up experiencing from home and parents. The tendency to adopt scripts from those around us is very apparent in the behavior of teenagers, who may too readily take on the scripts of their peers. Mentors in our lives influence us not so much from the specific instructions they might give us, but from the story line (script) that they both narrate and live out.

Stories can also heal. Narrative psychologist and researcher Dan McAdams suggests that a good autobiography can bring healing and growth via the process of meaningful personal integration.[9] He likens some forms of psychotherapy to retelling of a life with the therapeutic goal of depathologizing the client's life. This is also consistent with the work of social psychologist James Pennebaker who demonstrated that chronic stress can be buffered by having the person write a story about their stressful events in a logical and coherent manner.[10] As we described in Chapter 2, research suggests that attachment style can be transmitted intergenerationally – from parents to their children. However, researchers have also discovered that mothers who had insecure attachment styles as children can raise securely attached infants if they develop a coherent narrative – rich with meaning and logical in its telling – about their own upbringing.

The importance of narratives in our understanding of ourselves is illustrated in the rare neurological condition *dysnarrativia*, which is caused by damage to a particular part of the frontal lobe of the brain. Persons with dysnarrativia are impaired in their ability to formulate a narrative history of their thoughts and experiences, even though they are quite aware at the moment of their circumstances and thoughts. According to neurological researchers Kay Young and Jeffrey Saver, individuals with this disorder "lead 'denarrated' lives, aware but failing to organize experience in an action-generating temporal frame."[11] Most interestingly, these individuals are described as having lost their sense of self, suggesting a strong link between the capacity to narrate one's experiences and important qualities of personhood. Thus, it is not simply that narratives prompt us to imaginatively simulate behaviors and events described in stories, or provide the scripts for anticipating and organizing

---

[9] Dan McAdams, *The Stories We Live By: Personal Myth and the Making of the Self* (New York: William Morrow and Company, 1993).

[10] James W. Pennebaker, *Opening Up: The Healing Power of Expressing Emotions* (New York: Guilford Press, 1997).

[11] Kay Young and Jeffrey L. Saver, "The Neurology of Narrative," *Substance: A Review of Theory & Literary Criticism* 30, no. 1/2 (2001):78.

social behavior, but the narrative of our own history contributes significantly to our personhood.

Finally, utilizing the impact of story has always been a fundamental strategy of preaching. The major points in an effective sermon are accompanied by telling an illustrative story. Most congregants, if asked the next day about the sermon, are more likely to remember the illustrations than the explicit points of the sermon. But, as we have argued, we do not just remember the facts of the story abstractly, but tend to incorporate the actions and their consequences into our understanding of the world and our repertoire of potential behaviors. This, of course, is modulated by the preacher's positive or negative evaluation of the actions. Thus, a really good story typically has more impact on the congregation than a thoroughgoing exegesis of the meaning of a scriptural passage. Modern narrative theology is based on just this idea. The stories we know and carry around in our memories are fundamental to the way we act and think, and thus they constitute the theology that we actually live out. In Section III of this book, we take the concept of narrative one step further in describing how groups, including congregations, come to co-narrate a story about themselves that forms both the life of the group and the lives of the individuals within the group.

WISDOM AND VIRTUE

The desired outcome of Christian life is not simply conversion or belief, but continued growth in wisdom and virtue. Wisdom is more than merely knowing what is abstractly true, but includes judgment, discernment, and insight about how to act in various contexts.[12] Virtue is sometimes thought of as moral excellence, judged in terms of scrupulous compliance with absolute standards of right and wrong. However, virtue is not so much about behavior with respect to the extremes of the distribution of right or wrong actions, but mostly about the nuances of personal conduct. Both virtue and wisdom are critical in the daily demands posed by all of the complex situations that emerge from a life

---

[12] Warren S. Brown, "Discussion: Seven Pillars of the House of Wisdom," in R. Sternberg and J. Jordan, *A Handbook of Wisdom: Psychological Perspectives* (New York: Cambridge University Press, 2005), 353–368.

lived within a community of persons. Thus, it is hard to think of either virtue or wisdom separate from the other. It is also difficult, if not impossible, to abstract either wisdom or virtue as a quality of a particular individual apart from the ongoing, daily role the person plays within his or her social and interpersonal settings.

Philosopher Alasdair MacIntyre, in his book *Dependent Rational Animals*,[13] gives an account of the development of virtue and wisdom that focuses on their role in the flourishing of persons within communities. According to MacIntyre, people can flourish only in the context of their interdependence. MacIntyre's title, *Dependent Rational Animals*, is quite explicit in helping us understand this perspective. "Animals" refers to MacIntyre's view of humankind as continuous with the animal world and, therefore, essentially physical creatures in social contexts. This is a version of the view of human nature we proposed in the first part of this book. "Rational" expresses MacIntyre's understanding of the critical role of practical reasoning in fostering human flourishing. This form of rationality is not exactly the conscious, abstract sort of rationality we typically think of when we encounter this term. Rather, the rationality referred to by MacIntyre is more like common everyday wisdom and virtue. In the end, the goal of human development for MacIntyre is to become an "independent practical reasoner" – someone whom others would consider to be wise in their perspectives and virtuous in behavior. MacIntyre is pointing to something that is very much like the spiritual maturity and wisdom that we believe the church should be seeking to promote.

The critical step in becoming an independent practical reasoner – that is, a person of wisdom and virtue – is "acknowledged dependence" (thus, the designation of humans as "*dependent* rational animals"). MacIntyre's point is that only those persons who are continually able to acknowledge, and function within, their dependence on others are successful in becoming truly mature, virtuous, and wise – that is, independent practical reasoners. MacIntyre writes, ". . . the acquisition of the necessary virtues, skills, and self-knowledge is something that we in key part owe to those

[13] Alasdair MacIntyre, *Dependent Rational Animals: Why Human Beings Need the Virtues* (Chicago: Open Court, 1999).

particular others on whom we have had to depend."[14] This dependence is most critical for children, but continues throughout life in all forms of interpersonal interactions and attachments. MacIntyre continues, "For we continue to the end of our lives to need others to sustain us in our practical reasoning."

We are most particularly dependent on others for the feedback that allows for continued self-knowledge, helping us detect and correct our mental and moral errors – our lapses in wisdom and virtue. "From both types of mistake the best protections are friendship and collegiality."[15] In a conversation, a comment was made that another person was rather blunt, to which the response was offered, "We all need a few blunt friends." Well, perhaps not blunt, but at least friends who will compassionately inform us of our blunders, mistakes, and flaws of character. In terms of our model of humans as complex dynamical systems, compassionate feedback is a cushioned catastrophe that can cause us to reorganize and grow. Reciprocal imitation and shared narratives are also means of growth implicit in our interdependence.

Thus, Christian maturity and formation in wisdom and virtue are dependent on contexts of relationships with other persons – whether a secure and loving family when we are young children, a few adult mentors during adolescence, good friends and associates to imitate, the right sorts of narratives to live by, or a network of compassionately truthful Christian friends. We are formed into mature, virtuous, and wise persons, not by some disembodied mystical process, but by life together in a body of persons.

[14] MacIntyre, op. cit., 96.
[15] MacIntyre, op. cit.

6

ॐ

How We Are Changed and Transformed

THE MALFORMATION OF JANE

Jane reported that she didn't "feel in control of her life or herself." She had come to notice a persistent discrepancy between what she said she believed as a Christian and how she lived. For example, Jane believed it was important to "love God and to love your neighbor as yourself," but she continually found herself gossiping about others, being hurtful to friends and family, losing her temper, and even engaging in behaviors that violated her own Christian ethics. Jane would become aware of the discrepancy between her beliefs and behavior (often after the fact) and feel terribly guilty. Her typical cycle would be to act (her inappropriate behavior was always triggered by interpersonal interactions), feel regret and guilt, repent, and then, pulling herself up by the bootstraps, try to muster the willpower to do better next time. This never-ending cycle was not only leading Jane to social isolation, but to a growing sense of depression and hopelessness.

Throughout Part II, we have been describing how people develop and change. We enter the world as physically open and self-organizing systems, but also prewired for relating to other persons. Therefore, it is relationships that shape our process of self-organization. Through interpersonal experiences and imitation, we learn to interact with others, and, in the process, hopefully emerge as complete persons (fully capable of reciprocal loving relationships with others). As we continually interact with others, these reciprocal interactions become reinforced, creating habitual patterns that come to characterize our interpersonal interactions. If it is true that we are formed in and through relationships with

88

others, then it makes sense that it is also in and through relationships that we can be changed and transformed. In a nutshell, *we believe people change in, through, and with other people.*

Therefore, it is not enough to simply acquire new information about ourselves. To be reformed, we have to experience new forms of embodied, real-time, social interactions. We need to be impacted by different sorts of relational interactions, so that our self – that is, our *whole embodied way of being in the world* – is reshaped. We need new kinds of relational experiences, including opportunities and encouragement to try out new patterns of relating. What is more, human social behavior is always reciprocal – it includes both acting and being acted upon, observing and imitating the behavior of others as they observe and imitate us. Thus, in relationships we are jointly re-formed.

In this chapter, we will explore what is known about personal transformation as it is understood within the field of clinical psychology. We will particularly focus on group therapy, which has the most direct parallel with what might happen in congregations, particularly within small groups of Christians. We will also explore versions of these processes that occur within the very small scale, two-person encounters of individual therapy. We do not presume that the work of the church is merely psychotherapy, nor do we wish to argue for substituting psychotherapy for congregational life. Rather, we believe that, whatever else is going on, similar basic principles of human transformation apply in both psychological therapy and the transformative life of Christian congregations.

THE GOOD AND BAD OF UNCONSCIOUS HABITS

Research in both psychology and brain science suggests that through repeated exposures to similar kinds of interpersonal experiences, we develop anticipatory expectations. These expectations become linked to behavioral habits that are processed primarily at the level of emotions and unconscious appraisals. Subsequently, these emotional and behavioral responses can be triggered in new situations that the brain interprets as similar to the original experiences. Consequently, what we may subjectively experience and automatically do in this new situation sometimes seems mysterious, even to us. There seems to be no logical explanation for why we are feeling what we are feeling. Our learned relational templates created an automatic anticipation of the likely nature of this new interpersonal situation that unconsciously influences our perceptions and our behavior.

These unconscious processes are, in the majority of cases, socially appropriate and highly effective, but they also can be inadequate and socially ineffective. For example, if a person has a history of frequently being emotionally injured by a critical parent, when she encounters criticism from a new individual – even if it is delivered gently and in a constructive manner – she will likely have a general sense, dredged up from her past, that this new person is dangerous and untrustworthy. This sense of danger will cause her to reenact the learned patterns of behavior that were used in the past to protect her *self* from injury (for instance, distancing, becoming defensive, attacking back, or playing the martyr). Of course there is a very good chance that the other person is mystified by her reaction to the gentle criticism, and may also react with automatic behavior patterns for dealing with an overly defensive, emotional person. If the other's reaction is not calming, a destructive interactive cycle can begin. If this cycle is not broken in a constructive manner, there is a strong possibility that any relationship that might have existed is headed toward termination. Jane's problems described at the beginning of this chapter are of this type, although different in the detail of her life experience and the current forms of expression.

These sorts of habit-generated interpersonal scenarios are ubiquitous. Research suggests that such automatic reactions, involving unconsciously triggered appraisals and emotions prompting associated habitual behavior, may be enacted many times per day. In fact, because of our brain's limited capacity for attention and conscious information processing, researchers suggest that a majority of our daily behavior is initiated in this way, outside of our control or conscious awareness.[1] This means that we often don't know why we seem compelled to act in certain ways, or even how we have acted, until well after the fact, if ever at all.

All too often in churches, this sort of inappropriate response leads to a destructive relational cycle. Individuals often report that they left a

---

[1] John A. Bargh and Tanya L. Chartrand, "The Unbearable Automaticity of Being," *American Psychologist* 54, no. 7 (1999).

church because they were treated poorly or not made to feel welcome. While such problems certainly do occur at the congregational level (that is, a generally unfriendly and inhospitable congregational environment), it is also fairly easy to imagine that some of the injured feelings suffered at a particular church are, in fact, subjectively felt interpersonal appraisals, based as much on the person's prior history as on actual interactions. For example, it is not hard to imagine persons with a history of being rejected becoming angry with a busy and stressed pastor who appears not to have time for them. Such injured-feeling persons may then withdraw, making it harder for a pastor who is unaware of the perceived hurt to approach and relate with them in a normal fashion, leading to a cycle of poor interactions. They may then leave the church, blaming it all on the pastor. Without the capacity to recognize their own role in this interpersonal disconnect, they assume no personal responsibility.

HOPE FOR CHANGE

It is possible, though, that a different scenario may play out in transformative relationships. There are transformative interpersonal contexts in which, if potentially destructive emotional interpersonal responses occur, they do not prompt reactions that confirm the inappropriate expectations and do not launch the relationship into a destructive cycle. In good therapy, in healthy groups and congregations, and in some kinds of friendships, the other person (say, therapist or friend) does not leave, disengage, or react in kind, and, thus, the person's anticipatory expectations are disconfirmed. In this way, the person learns that whatever his or her worst fear might have been, it did not come to fruition. Although the situation may have looked and felt just like ones that once burned the person, the situation didn't in fact burn – it was not even hot. Sometimes this process becomes conscious – or "talk about-able" – which can be very powerful in opening opportunities for change. More frequently, a latent unconscious process of change happens in the form of: trigger $\rightarrow$ inappropriate response $\rightarrow$ disconfirmation of belief $\rightarrow$ reinforcement of change. In either case, a new kind of interpersonal scenario has taken place and, if given the chance for repetition, a new interpersonal template will begin to form.

This is one of the central change mechanisms of healthy groups. The very nature of transformative groups, which are composed of a small number of individuals committed to long-term interacting to learn about themselves in relationship to others, ensures that interpersonal templates *will be* triggered, but because of the ongoing commitment to stay working together, inappropriate and destructive interpersonal habits can be changed. It is not only the new experience that can transform an interpersonal emotional template; what really solidifies the change is the individual beginning to behave differently. A new way of responding confirms a new experience and cements it in the person's bodily systems as a new kind of interpersonal emotional template and behavioral habit.

PROCESSES OF TRANSFORMATION IN SMALL GROUPS

Intentional involvement in long-term small groups is often the place where a change process can best occur. Many psychotherapists now postulate that most psychological problems that are not primarily biological in nature are interpersonal, or at least have significant interpersonal consequences. Therefore, such problems may best be treated in richly interpersonal group settings. These groups may be therapy groups facilitated by a trained and licensed professional, or peer-led groups (such as Alcoholics Anoymous, Narcotics Anonymous, or Celebrate Recovery). Group situations that are transformative must present persons with opportunities for real, immediate, and authentic interpersonal interactions. In such group settings, members can obtain immediate feedback on how their behavior impacts others and have the opportunity to practice in-vivo new kinds of behaviors based on that feedback. Importantly, members can also come to appreciate how *others impact them*, what they feel, and how they tend to behave when triggered in various interpersonal ways.

Psychotherapist, author, and professor Irving Yalom[2] has written one of the definitive books on group therapy, now in its fifth edition. In his work and research with groups, he has outlined eleven curative factors in group therapy: *instillation of hope, universality, imparting of information,*

[2] Irving Yalom, *The Theory and Practice of Group Psychotherapy*, 5th ed. (New York: Basic Books, 2005).

altruism, corrective recapitulation of the primary family group, development of socializing techniques, imitative behavior, interpersonal learning, group cohesiveness, catharsis, and existential factors. Group experiences are potentially transformative because of the interactions of these eleven factors, that are typically operative in various nonlinear combinations during the course of a transformative group experience.

Hope is essential in bringing about change in individuals. Motivation, which is related to hope, is a great predictor of whether or not psychological interventions will be successful. Group experiences, in which members encounter other individuals who are farther along the journey, can help them develop hope – hope in the form of imagination for how they might change and develop, and for the kinds of communities within which they might thrive. Universality is the feeling that "I am not alone and not the only one to ever struggle with this problem." This realization usually brings a great sense of relief and normalization. While groups certainly do impart new information, other factors are usually more powerful. Through imitation, members have the opportunity to try out new ways of acting and responding, such as altruistic interactions with members of the group. While members typically join a group to receive something, they may actually grow most themselves as they begin to engage in benevolent sharing with the members of the group, fostered by imitation. This connects with Yalom's concept of interpersonal learning and the development of socialization. Persons often do not truly know how they impact others in loving and beneficial ways – or in unloving and malevolent ways. Rather, they may spend much of their time in narcissistic obsessions about how others are affecting them! In groups that are characterized by immediacy, authenticity, and candor, members can receive direct feedback about their own behavior and how it impacts others. Members are caught by others in loving and unloving behavior and, through feedback, slowly develop the ability to be self-observant. Over time this capacity for self-observation allows individuals to recognize their actions and begin to behave differently.

The important point is that change comes about in groups by providing its members a supportive and nonthreatening environment in which to gain a different sort of social experience. When all goes well, the group experience allows members the opportunity to develop new patterns of appraisal, emotion, and behavior in social situations.

Two basic commitments are necessary for this kind of change to be possible in small groups. First, individuals must commit themselves to relationships in a manner that communicates, "I am in this for the long haul." Replacing old emotional, interpersonal, and behavioral patterns with new ones requires repeated exposure to new experiences. If a person leaves the group every time relationships become messy, his or her feelings are hurt, or things get uncomfortable, change will not occur in that individual. This applies both in therapy and in the church. The second mechanism necessary for transformation is the opportunity and commitment to speak into one another's life. That is, permission must be given, as it is in group therapy, to comment on one another's present behavior and its impact, but within the context of love and support.

To anticipate what we will consider later with respect to the church, it is unfortunate that most small groups found within church settings are not transformative in the manner we are describing. The reasons for this are multiple, but we offer a few hypotheses. First, the objectives of these groups tend to focus on pleasant social interactions and acquisition of abstract information, such as Bible study, rather than a deeper life lived together in communal relationships with the goal of spiritual and character formation. Consequently, these groups develop neither the sort of shared language and story nor the group skills necessary to bring about true transformation, such as the curative factors identified by Yalom. Second, most groups do not develop covenants hallmarked by candor as in feedback and confession, authenticity as in speaking the truth in love, confidentiality as in respecting integrity of persons and group, and safety as in love. Third, without a covenant commitment, these groups do not stay together long enough for important transformative practices to occur.

HOW JANE UNDERGOES CHANGE

We now return to the story of Jane, which opened the chapter. Using this example we will illustrate more specficially the processes necessary to bring about transformation. The example is not an effort to promote one particular form of intervention (for example, psychotherapy), but rather an attempt to demonstrate the processes we believe necessary for change. This process of change is contrasted with typical models that are often evident in the church where some form of disembodied spiritual experience is presumed to be sufficient.

Jane's usual cycle of habitual forms of inadequate response triggered in interpersonal interactions (that is, regret, guilt and shame, repentance, and willpower to act differently) repeated itself countless times, leading to growing frustration and creeping despair. She finally decided she needed help, so she went to her pastor. Her pastor agreed with Jane that there was a problem and diagnosed it as a spiritual problem of sin and the impurity of her heart. If Jane would get her heart right with God – confess her sin and repent – he told her that her life would change. He prescribed prayer and study of the scriptures. What he didn't seem to recognize was that Jane had been trying this approach for years. While this somewhat abstract, individualist, and internally directed intervention had helped her consciously see the sinfulness of her ways and provided some solace, it had not freed her from her frustrating cycle of behavior. This intervention was not wrong, but was incomplete, in that it was not sufficiently embodied and relational to bring about real personal transformation.

So, feeling that what her pastor offered her was insufficient, Jane sought out - a certified spiritual director. The director's diagnosis and "treatment" also tended toward being inward and disembodied. The director suggested that Jane needed to reorient her relationship to God, deepening it and learning to listen to God. The director prescribed centering prayer and *lectio divina* – a form of meditative reading of scripture – as well as several other classic spiritual disciplines. Although Jane found all of this helpful for growing in knowledge and even gaining an emotionally felt greater intimacy with God, she nevertheless continued to struggle with gaining mastery of her behavior. Finally, as a last ditch effort, she sought out a Christian therapist.

Jane's first therapist listened empathically and, as far as she could sense, didn't force on her any particular understanding of her problems. Because this therapist was such a good listener and genuinely liked her, it was easy for Jane to form a strong attachment with her. Her therapist believed, and communicated to Jane, that the source of her problems was a wrong and inadequate way of thinking. Jane suffered from faulty thoughts about herself, others, and the way the world worked. What Jane needed to do was to rethink her life, herself, and others – to move from faulty understandings to more true beliefs.

The therapy helped Jane for some time. She indeed did have faulty ideas about how relationships functioned and what sort of person she was. By working on her inner world of cognitions, Jane began to feel some initial relief from some of the chaos she seemed to find – actually created – within herself. But, the therapy eventually began to outlive its usefulness. While Jane had a better understanding of how her thought life corrupted her relationships and at times was better able to soothe herself when she was feeling insecure or upset, she was still unable to genuinely connect with other persons. In fact, her therapy seemed to have inadvertently pushed her toward a kind of cool detachment. If she had all "her stuff" together and she still couldn't connect, then she was left with only one conclusion: It must be the other person's issues.

While this conclusion might have exonerated Jane from personal responsibility she began to recognize that not all her problems could realistically be the fault of others. So Jane then did what many individuals will do in this situation – she went to a new therapist! With the new therapist, Jane began to explore her history. She was the baby of five children born to older parents who were both fatigued by parenting and deeply entrenched in their careers. For these reasons, and some intense sibling rivalry, Jane grew up anxiously attached, feeling lonely and invisible. She learned in her family of origin that to be heard she had to throw a tantrum or at least make some kind of a scene. Although she was not cognizant of it, she carried this feeling of being invisible and detached into adolescence, where it became more salient by her anticipation of social rejection. Because of this interpersonal template, Jane frequently felt misunderstood, left out, and mistreated. However, when triggered by certain kinds of situations, she would respond with anger (that is, an adult version of a tantrum). This interpersonal style, coupled with Jane's low self-worth, caused Jane to engage in behaviors of which she was only partially aware. These behaviors were based on what she unconsciously believed was necessary in order for her to obtain or maintain connections (that is, attachments) with others. At times these ways of acting meant sacrificing her sexual ethics in order to be seen and "cared" for. At other times, she might engage in hurtful behavior toward one person in order to gain the favor of another, for example, using gossip. Through the therapeutic process of self-discovery, she began to understand how, even though she gave intellectual assent to certain Christian values, her developmental history and subsequent relational templates were affecting her attitudes and behaviors in ways that were directly at odds with her beliefs.

Although this new understanding was necessary, it was not sufficient to bring about complete change in Jane. The transformative factor was not something that occurred *within* Jane but what occurred *between* the therapist and Jane. Jane began to experience a *new kind of relationship* with her therapist. It was clear to her that this therapist understood her, but also didn't give up on her as friends often did, even when she at times lashed out at the therapist because of some imagined rejection , such as when she started the session five minutes late. The way in which her therapist interacted with Jane was a new kind of relating that began to shape her in different ways. In this new interpersonal scenario between Jane and her therapist, Jane began to act differently. Early in the therapy, Jane interacted with the therapist in much the same way she interacted with all individuals by paying little attention to her therapist except to monitor her for signs of rejection. However, Jane eventually was able to step outside her own self-preoccupation and see her therapist as a real person with feelings who interacted with her differently than she expected. Jane's therapist provided her direct and authentic feedback on her behavior, even how it impacted her as therapist. This began to force Jane's self-observational capacity to develop. Jane began to imitate her therapist's genuine, caring, and authentic way of interacting with others when she was outside of therapy. The new interpersonal scenario that was developing in the context of the relationship between Jane and her therapist was reshaping Jane's way of interacting with others outside of therapy.

Let's take this imaginary, but all too common, scenario just a bit further. Let's imagine that Jane's last therapist did not see persons as dual entities, but as *whole-embodied-persons-embedded-in-the-world-of-relationships*. Thus, she believed that Jane would need many more than the one new kind of relationship she had experienced in therapy. And because Jane's therapist was a Christian, she felt it was imperative that Jane seek out other reciprocally shaping relationships, particularly a small group where the Kingdom of God was being lived out in community. In the right kind of church community, others would serve as models, reciprocal partners in Christian growth, and mirrors to Jane, providing her with opportunities to act and relate differently. The right kind of community experience could provide the sort of group curative factors discussed above, such as interpersonal feedback, hope, group cohesiveness and socialization. Such a community would indeed progressively transform her and she them.

MODELS OF CHANGE

We hope it is becoming clear that certain qualities of interpersonal interaction are what promote change and transformation of persons. Therefore, what we are not suggesting is merely a church Bible study and prayer group, a time-limited thematic group focused on a helpful book, or a group structured for those dealing with some specific problem, such as parenting. What we are envisioning is a small group of Christian individuals, ideally from different walks of life, committed to regularly meeting together for a more extended time, with the expressed purpose of helping one another grow as Christians and living out the Kingdom of God in embodied and behavioral ways. While prayer and Bible study would naturally be a part, this kind of group would also incorporate many of the curative factors identified by Yalom with respect to therapy groups. For example, Jane could experience universality when she became aware that she is not the only person who struggles interpersonally. She would receive hope as she witnessed others growing, and she would certainly learn new ways of socializing. And if her group were characterized by immediacy, authenticity, and candor, she would almost certainly receive feedback on how her behavior impacted others. In the context of these new experiences, Jane would find the freedom to begin to imitate the positive behavior exemplified by others in the group and to begin to receive by giving in the form of compassion and care for others. Sadly, these groups are difficult to find in most churches. This is one reason why most church members have to look for these kinds of transformative interpersonal experiences outside the church, in group therapy, for example.

What we have attempted to contrast through this example is two essentially different models of change. The models are based on different implicit perspectives of what it means to be a person. The first, exemplified by the pastor, spiritual director, and first therapist, is an approach based on a dualist, inner-outer (body-soul or body-mind) distinction where the inner world of Jane was set off from her physical being, social behavior, and interpersonal context. The second model, exemplified by the final therapist (and potentially the right kind of congregational setting), understood Jane as an embodied and socially embedded person. Thus, intervention was outer and relational, with the goal being to reshape automatic social and behavioral patterns.

In the first model, Jane's unexamined view of human nature, like those of her pastor, spiritual director, and first therapist, caused her to understand her problems in terms of an inner soul, self, or mind. Consequently, the process of change was focused on something entirely inside her as an autonomous, individual person, and only secondarily related to her social relationships or physical existence. In essence, they attempted to help her obtain the proper inner knowledge she needed through prayer, Bible study, or thinking consciously about aspects of her life to bring her health and healing. Although there is undoubtedly an important place for these kinds of interventions and religious disciplines, they are only partially helpful when they are decontextualized from a person's physical being as embedded in interpersonal relationships.

In contrast, the final experience of therapy was successful in beginning to reshape Jane's automatic and habitual social patterns in ways not readily available to her thinking and conscious awareness. A new type of relationship began to progressively reshape Jane's ways of interacting with people. It was not so much what was said, or even what Jane was thinking, but the quality of the interpersonal relationship that was being experienced. Significant transformation began to occur as Jane began to adopt new ways of interacting and to carry this change around with her. A new attachment style was created which brought about changes that were evident in the quality of interactions that occurred between her and other persons.

Thus, significant personal transformation occurs when persons come to experience themselves as embodied persons who were shaped, and continued to be shaped, in and through an interconnected web of personal relationships. It is generally a distraction from genuine transformation to view persons as an inner self (the "real me" inside), rather than as a constantly reforming amalgamation of all their interactions from birth to the present (that is, a dynamical system). What transformation requires is not some kind of inward special knowledge or subjective experience, be it spiritual or psychological, but new kinds of relationships that reshape relational patterns. Jane needed to experience herself as an interpersonal "reciprocating self"[3] who is shaped by interpersonal interactions and thus in turn can participate in the transformation of others.

In this excursion into forms and experiences of psychotherapy, it is not our intention to defend a particular form of therapy, or even therapy at all. The important point is to illustrate, using a fictitious although not entirely unfamiliar example, how people change and are reshaped. We firmly believe that faith communities that come to embody this more bodily and relational view of persons – shedding the view of persons as constituted primarily of hidden inner selves or souls – become more open to engaging in restorative relationships, similar to that we have described in this example of therapy. We will say more about this in later chapters, but let it suffice for now to say that we value small groups of believers who see their role not solely as the acquisition of new special or spiritual knowledge or as restoring the inner souls of each individual through inner affective experiences, but rather as embodying a form of interpersonal sharing and shaping that is reciprocally transformative. This takes a kind of community commitment that goes beyond a typical Bible study or prayer group, even though these forms of Christian discipline are critical to the life of such a group. Thus, while many of the spiritual disciplines that have been handed down over the centuries can be helpful in this kind of transformative change, these disciplines must be contextualized within an embodied and communal understanding of persons who are shaped and transformed by being nested within reciprocating transformative relationships. When spiritual disciplines become divorced from this understanding and become nothing more than inwardly focused exercises of autonomous individuals, we believe they lose their primary power for fostering Christian growth and maturity. It is not that therapy has discovered something that the church has never known. Rather, therapy has merely repackaged something that our modern individualistic society and our Gnostic religious tendencies have lost.

---

[3] Jack O. Balswick, Pamela Ebstyne King, and Kevin S. Reimer, *The Reciprocating Self: Human Development in Theological Perspective* (Downers Grove, IL: IVP, 2005).

∾

PART III

EMBODIED CHRISTIAN LIFE AND

THE CHURCH: RETROSPECT AND

PROSPECT

REVIEW

In Part II we described the development, formation, and change of persons. Our primary objective was to bring to the forefront those things known to be the case in human neuroscience and psychology that should be kept in mind as we consider the formation of Christian persons from the perspective of an embodied view of human nature.

Chapter 4 focused on children, summarizing important issues in their mental and social development. An important part of this process is the maturation of the physical structure of the brain. Because of the unusual openness and plasticity of the developing human brain, social influences are particularly critical to the direction of the development of personhood. Thus, we described the impact of interpersonal interactions such as imitation, shared attention, attachment, and empathy, as well as the formative nature of language and story.

Equally important for understanding Christian formation are the dynamics of continuing adult personality and character development. Thus, Chapter 5 dealt with adult formation and transformation. Using the descriptive language of dynamical systems, we gave an account of how adults are continually changed and transformed for better or worse as they experience life. We paralleled our summary of child development by describing how formative forces in adults are still almost exclusively interpersonal – including, as with children, imitation, attachments, and life-forming narratives. In the end, what is at stake in adult development is the degree to which wisdom and virtue come to characterize persons.

Finally, Chapter 6 brought to bear on this discussion of formation, the important dynamics of therapeutic change in persons with inadequate developmental histories. Here we leaned heavily on what can be gleaned from the theory and practice of counseling and psychotherapy. Again, the critical processes that induce transformation are the quality of inter-personal relationships.

PREVIEW

In Part III, the final section of this book, we take the view of human nature as physical and embodied, as described in Part I, and the implications of this view for the formation of persons, as dealt with in Part II. We use them to create a renewed understanding of the life of the church and its role in the transformation of persons. So much of contemporary congregational life and worship are rooted in a distinc-tion between body and soul. The question we attempt to answer is, What should churches be like if persons are physically embodied and socially embedded?

Chapter 7 attempts to answer this question from the point of view of individual Christian persons. Why do embodied persons need a church body in order to become mature – that is, persons of Christian virtue and wisdom? To answer this question, we revisit issues such as dynamic openness, attachment, imitation and narrative, but now in the context of Christian persons who are members of a congregation.

In Chapter 8, we consider the nature of the church itself as the Body of Christ. We discuss here how a church is shaped and grows. A valuable perspective in this section is the view of the church as genuine body – a view that is given credibility by considering the church to be a dynamical system (much as we viewed individual persons as dynamical systems). The relationship between catastrophe and church growth is central to this discussion. Group size and group time are also critical to a trans-formative life together.

Finally, Chapter 9 looks even more deeply at the nature of the narra-tive around which the church is formed. What sort of story does a church tell itself, and how does that particular story affect its growth as the Body of Christ, as well as the formation of congregants? We also consider the issue of the nature of worship when considered from the viewpoint of a congregation of embodied and socially embedded persons. We end this chapter with a discussion of human disability as a case in point about story, formation, and ministry within the Body of Christ.

7

∾

Why Bodies Need Churches

The Sunday morning scene was familiar. As Sally attempted to get herself and the children ready and dressed for church, her husband Phil leisurely sipped his coffee and read the paper dressed in shorts and hiking boots. While Sally and the kids would spend the morning at church, Phil would be up hiking in the foothills. This was a pattern they had developed over the years and Sally had learned to rarely challenge the arrangement, but this particular morning she felt compelled.

"Why don't you come to church with us this week?" she asked sweetly.

"Hon, we have been through this a thousand times. You go to church and I go hiking," Phil responded.

"But I don't go to church for fun or exercise, I go for spiritual reasons," Sally retorted.

"That is exactly why I go hiking. I have told you that before. I feel more spiritual in the mountains. Communing with nature is a religious experience for me."

"Going to the mountains is not the same as going to church" Sally said.

"Why not?"

"It just isn't; everybody knows that."

Phil paused, breathed deeply, and asked, "Tell me again why you go to church?"

"Well," Sally hesitated, "I get closer to God there. I learn about him and grow in my faith journey."

"You keep using the same argument over and over," responded Phil. "By your definition of church, I am experiencing the same thing in the

mountains every week that you experience in church. I can do exactly what you are doing in church by myself in the foothills. I experience God there, through nature, and subsequently grow spiritually. I am quieted and centered there. I am a better person because I hike weekly! Until you can show me how church is uniquely different, I don't see any reason to put on uncomfortable clothes and sit in a state of boredom two hours every week."

"Well hiking isn't church, no matter what you say," Sally said, not hiding her exasperation.

"The mountains are my church and I'd love to have you and the kids come to my church every Sunday, but I don't make you feel guilty when you don't want to come," he chided. Phil kissed her gently on the cheek as he headed out the door.

WHY GO TO CHURCH?

While many who are reading this book might not consider heading to the mountains a substitute for church, nevertheless, we may be hard pressed to help Sally give Phil a good reason why church is different from hiking. What is the point of church?

So far throughout this book we have been considering the implications of the idea that persons are not an immaterial immortal soul temporarily inhabiting a physical body, but rather are *whole-embodied-persons-embedded-in-the-world*. If this is true, then we need to reconsider the nature of spiritual growth and development in light of this view. The tendency to see ourselves as two distinct parts, only one of which is relevant to Christian life, has implications for the way in which we conceptualize church. It may also trap us in a dead end in our Christian journey without a viable path for growing more like Christ.

Another version of Phil and Sally's confusion about church would be the perspective of the typical "church shopper." Take Mike for example.

Mike, a young post-college twenty-something, is an incorrigible church shopper. While in college, when he attended church he chose whichever college program was providing the best food, had the best music, and the prettiest girls. Since he graduated, he has been looking for a church that fits his preferences and feels right. He wants to attend a church where he will be "fed." He frequently speaks about wanting to find a particular kind of "worship experience" that feeds him spiritually and that "refuels his batteries" for the coming week.

Mike has a consumer's model of church attendance that is, "Find a church that meets my personal spiritual needs." Mike illustrates an understanding of church that is based on an individualist ideal about spirituality that grants precedence to his own inward experience. Focused on the quality of his own individual experiences, his approach is not unlike finding the form of entertainment that gives him the biggest emotional charge. He is looking for a church that does for him what hiking does for Phil.

In fact, this view of the church is not at all unusual. Many churches now refer to what occurs during worship as *worship experiences* rather than *worship services* – which semantically codes an interesting difference in ways we might engage in worship: serving versus experiencing. The idea of a worship experience implies that going to church is for the purpose of renewing a subjective inward experience. According to this view, we attend for something that we hope to receive. For each person it is about "me" – what the person gets out of it and how it impacts him or her. What we are to *do* with the experience is not entirely clear, and often beside the point! The danger in this perspective is that church becomes no more than what Bono, lead singer of the rock band U2, calls "Bless Me Clubs."

Sally has a similar sentimental view of church as church shopper Mike, although she has settled into a particular church. Other than how church makes her feel, she can't quite conceive, let alone explain to her husband, why church is vitally important, not to mention why it is different from his solitary spiritual experience alone in the mountains. The reason Sally can't defend the importance of church is because she has the same basic understanding of spirituality as Phil – and Mike. For all three, spirituality is anchored in internal sentimental experiences, which are presumed to cause one to grow in some ethereal way. That is, they all understand spiritual growth to happen in solitary ways through certain forms of inner experience. But, if this is all that church amounts to, then maybe the mountains are as good as church, or, if we are going to attend church, we should "shop" until we find a church that offers the kind of experience that gives each of us individually what are seeking.

We described in Chapter 2 the conclusion reached by many observers that the modern church has lapsed into the ancient heresy of Gnosticism. That is, Christian faith has become entirely a matter of special spiritual knowledge to be acquired by individual persons via certain kinds of inner experiences. In this understanding, the idea of spiritual specifically excludes anything material, physical or embodied. Sally, Phil, and Mike are all operating out of a Gnostic view of faith and the church – it is all about their own private inner spiritual experiences, to be sought out individually. These private inward spiritual experiences have little to do with relationships with other persons or embodied daily life in the world.

So, the question we wish to pursue in this chapter is the nature of spiritual formation and transformation of persons. Is it correct to conceive of this process as individual, private, and inner? If not, then how should we think of formation and the role the church plays? What might be an alternative view that provides a robust path to effectual formation of persons? This chapter focuses on individual persons within the church, and in the following chapter we speak from the perspective of the nature of churches and congregations as a whole.

THE PURPOSE OF CHURCH

Before describing the formation of Christian persons, it is helpful to consider various views of the purpose of the church. There are three that readily come to mind. First, there is the idea of bringing individuals into a committed and personal relationship with God (often spoken of as conversion or salvation) through the witness of the church and proclamation of the gospel. Another goal often expressed is that the church should help persons become mature as Christians. This second goal is also sometimes described as the sanctification of believers in that persons become increasingly holy in their life and personhood. Finally, the purpose of the church is also described by some as the formation of a community of persons that is characterized by the reign of God and, as such, reflects God's presence as a means of grace to the world. This last goal is less prominent in descriptions of the church, mostly because the specifics of such a congregation are harder to imagine. However, very generally, the goal of this kind of congregation is a life characterized by reciprocal hospitality and love that shapes the lives of its members and functions actively in the surrounding community as a representation of, and a message about, the presence and activity of God.

Each of these goals forms some part of the overall mission of the church. However, these goals look somewhat different when we understand persons as whole and embodied rather than as two-part (body-soul) creatures. For example, a body-soul dualist might conceptualize salvation as a mystical change in the status of the nonmaterial, inner part of the person. The soul has a new status and is now destined for heaven. But a more holistic and embodied view of persons would consider salvation as turning of the whole person toward Christ – a bodily and behavioral change and reorientation involving a change of the entire person in relationship to the whole of God's physical and social creation. The whole embodied person is redeemed and transformed.

In the fanciful stories in this chapter, all three characters share a common misunderstanding of the nature of the second goal of the church – maturation and growth as Christians. Sally, Phil, and Mike each conceive of their Christian life and maturity as individual, private, and inner, and, therefore, maturity is measured by the quality of their subjective experiences. To grow in Christ is to have more consistent and intense periods of subjective feelings that are interpreted as evidence of the presence of God. While such times may come and have value in the development of persons, focusing on these experiences as the *sole* means of growth is to fall victim to the sort of misthinking that was being promoted by the Gnostics who plagued the early church. This early heresy was all about seeking a deeper Christian life through special spiritual knowledge (gnosis) gained by inner mystical experiences. If this is the means of Christian growth, then sitting in a pew absorbing the religious ambience, or going to a mountain top, or shopping around for the church that provides the greatest emotional buzz all make perfect sense.

The alternative is the view that spiritual formation is about reshaping the whole embodied person – as in new habits, a different character, new virtues, and a greater capacity for hospitality, love, and care for others. In this more embodied view, Christian growth and sanctification are understood, not in terms of the status of the soul, but as the whole person gaining in Christian wisdom and virtue. Thus, Paul's reference to "Christ in you" (Col. 1:27 NIV) would not be so much a description of the mystical presence of Christ inside our bodies, but a reshaping of our whole physical-mental-psychological selves into the image and likeness of Christ. This sort of reshaping of whole persons is unlikely to happen while one is merely sitting in a pew or on a mountain top. This sort of growth happens in the embodied and embedded give-and-take of the ongoing life of a highly interactive community of Christians.

This brings us to the third purpose of the church – the formation of a community of persons that is characterized by, and thus makes visible, the reign of God as a means of grace to the world and growth for its members. We would argue that this conceptualization of church transcends and subsumes the other two views. This sort of community is a proclamation and draws seekers. John 13:35 states, "By this everyone will know that you are my disciples, if you love one another (NIV)." It is in and through both the communal and missional life of congregations that the world can come to know that God's reign is real and active. But congregations also powerfully shape the lives of all the participants. Individual growth is a by-product of congregational growth. Individuals grow in holiness as the community of Christians grows. Sally, Phil, and Mike all view church as a source of inner spiritual experiences and, thus, miss the point of church as a formative community. In what follows, we attempt to convey how formation of Christian persons can take place within congregations.

THE SOCIAL FORMATION OF PERSONS

We described how children are formed into persons in Chapter 4 and how adults change in Chapters 5 and 6. If we are indeed *whole-embodied-persons-embedded-in-the-world*, rather than two-part beings – body and soul – then our Christian formation occurs in a manner similar to child development and adult change. While our primary point may have been sufficiently clear in these prior chapters, let us be explicit by reiterating our critical assertion: *We believe people develop and change in, through, and with other people!* Consequently, we believe Christian formation takes place in, through, and with other Christians!

Since the processes of human formation are primarily social, spiritual formation in the Church is also social and interpersonal. We are formed by Christ *operating through his body*, the church – specific congregations of people who meet regularly in his name and share life together. Christ is mediated through all of creation, but most specifically through the body that is constituted by the persons who gather as the church. It is within the communal and missional life of a congregation that persons grow in the faith and are formed into mature Christians. A well-functioning community of Christians forms and brings to the fore wisdom and virtues in its members as these qualities are required by the community in living out its mission.

Therefore, to understand the nature of a church that is effective in forming people, we need to look again at the specifics of human formation as we described them in the previous chapters, but now viewed from the specific context of the church. What follows is a revisitation of these social and interpersonal forces of change, specifically as they operate in the lives of Christians within the context of the church.

At this point, many readers may be wondering about the role of personal devotions in the context of the sort of social formation we are proposing. We do not mean to be understood as devaluing personal devotions in any way. However, these solitary forms of worship must be viewed as firmly nested within, and emerging from, the community life and worship of the church. First, it is the church that teaches the groundwork for our interpretation of the scriptures we read, and it is the church that teaches us how to pray and what to pray for. What is done individually is an extension of what occurs corporately. Second, the primary outcome of the devotional life of an individual is enrichment of the life of the community through what the individual has to offer the whole congregation. Far from being a private, autonomous spiritual activity that nurtures the inner soul, physically embodied and socially embedded personal devotions would be directed outward toward God and to the Body of Christ in which the person participates.

THE DYNAMIC OPENNESS OF PERSONS

As we described previously, both adults and children are open physical systems able to be formed and reformed by interactions with their surrounding physical and social environment. Our genes bestow on us what is mostly just a vague set of preprogrammed predispositions and tendencies, but because of the flexible and plastic nature of the kind of physical system that constitutes human beings, we are continually open to change and reformation, even as adults (Thank God!).

Physiologically, this dynamic flexibility and openness to change is related to the fact that the interconnectedness of most brain cells (neurons) is continually open to change. Connections can come and go, or are strengthened or weakened, based on ongoing brain activity, as a person continually interacts with the world. New networks form, existing networks get modified, and some old networks disappear from disuse. This flexibility and openness is particularly true of the brains of children and adolescents, which not only have flexible connections, but are also physically developing (changing in the number, distribution, and characteristics of cells). Behaviorally, we call these changes learning and memory. But by these terms we cannot restrict our view to the learning and memory of facts or life events, but we must include the learning of ways of doing things (skills and habits) and of motivations and emotions (implicit positive and negative evaluations, degrees and qualities of attachments, values, likes and dislikes, loves and hates, relational memories).

In previous chapters, we used the theory of dynamical systems to describe how our flexible body and brain physiology comes to incorporate the high-level human mental properties of thinking, remembering, knowing, believing, choosing, and having inner subjective experiences. The dynamic flexibility of the interconnected functioning of the massive network of nerve cells that compose the brain allows it to organize itself to meet its environment and continually reorganize as new challenges are faced. A computer has to be fed a preset program. A brain programs and reprograms itself as it goes. The most important aspect of the environment that the brain programs itself to meet is the sophisticated interpersonal, social, cultural, and linguistic nature of our lives.

We also described how such systems are prompted to form and reform by catastrophes. This is a metaphorical term used to denote situations in human life in which the current formation of our self is no longer able to deal adequately with the circumstances at hand. We are consequently forced to either escape the situation or allow ourselves to be reformed. For Saul, the experience on the Damascus road was a huge catastrophe that forced his whole self (worldview, beliefs, behaviors, social networks, and so forth) into reformation. We also get a glimpse in the book of Acts of how the community of believers in Damascus guided and supported Saul through the processes of adaptation and reformation brought on by the personal catastrophe of an entirely new experience of Jesus, whose followers he had been persecuting. In a similar but less dramatic manner, it was Jane's experience (Chapter 6) with a therapist and with a group of Christians that played the role of both the source of catastrophe (the catalyst for change) and the support and guidance necessary throughout the process of growth and reformation. Thus, while some of these catastrophes are dramatic like Saul's, most are more subtle and engender a process of progressive change, like Jane's experience.

Thus, the first principle of Christian formation is the dynamic openness of persons, allowing flexibility, adaptability, and reformation of our selves in the light of new circumstance where our previous habits, emotions, and perspectives prove to be inadequate. The accompanying principle is that change comes about in the context of major or minor catastrophes. We do not grow in the context of continued comfort, harmony, and sameness.

THE ROLE OF SECURE ATTACHMENTS IN FORMATION

Our openness as persons and the reformations that take place in us from time to time in the face of catastrophes are a fundamental aspect of our human nature and its vast complexity and adaptability. But what is it that causes catastrophes to sometimes result in significant growth and sometimes elicit resistance to growth or engender the wrong sort of change?

Previously we noted how secure versus insecure forms of attachment in children influence the likelihood that they will explore new situations and easily meet new friends. Similarly as adults, our feelings of security or insecurity in relationships influence our openness to explore new situations, new ideas, and alternative ways of acting, reacting, and interacting. In the face of catastrophes created by confronting either our inadequacies or new challenges, whether or not we feel secure in our relationships with at least a few significant others influences our openness to change – less secure attachment results in greater rigidity and less openness to change and reorganization.

So also it is within a church congregation. The willingness of persons to take risks and venture into new and richer forms of community life, or unique forms of ministry that can be the catalyst for growth, is related to the degree to which members of the congregation feel secure in their relationships with one another. If interpersonal relations are shallow or, even worse, characterized by rivalry, jealousy, envy, or snobbish cliques, then few will venture into risky new avenues of friendship, ministry, or kingdom life that involve challenge and might foster growth. Everyone becomes rigidly frozen by insecurity. No one will risk entering into risky situations that might produce or exacerbate catastrophe, nor are they able to lean into, rather than escape, the catastrophe-producing situations that will inevitably occur.

Congregations are constituted by complex interactions between the life of the congregation itself and the preexisting attachment experiences and habits of each individual. Individuals bring their preexisting attachment styles to church. The characteristics of the life of the congregation can either reform or reinforce an insecure attachment style that would react to catastrophe with rigidity. Long-term, loving, and hospitable congregational relations can provide a basis for risk, growth, and new depths of spiritual formation. In turn, significant ministry and richer community life become possible when each person feels known and appreciated as a part of a congregation of Christians who are on a significant journey together.

Fostering secure relationships that provide the foundation for adventure and change takes *greater time* spent with *smaller groups* than is characteristic of the life of many modern congregations (whether the churches themselves are large or small). The formation of secure attachment requires a sufficient amount of quality time spent with the same group in a wide range of contexts. It is not that such relationships are easy or without conflict. Rather, there must come to exist sufficient depth of commitment and security with one another that will allow conflict or difference to resolve into growth. In the previous chapter, we saw how Jane was able to begin to make significant progress in her personal life in the context of a group where she felt a sense of consistent love and support.

Difficulty finding such relationships in modern society may be one of the reasons for the rise of psychotherapy. The mantra of many psychotherapists is, "It is the relationship that heals." Good therapists know, and clinical research bears this out, that a positive outcome of therapy is highly dependent on the quality of the therapist-patient relationship. Effective therapy can be difficult and at times conflictual (just like good friendships), but these difficult times are transformative if a secure relationship has been established. Jane would not have been able to do the difficult work she did in confronting her own inadequacies and allowing transformation if she did not believe that her therapist, and later her group, were committed to her – good and bad. Growth and formation of persons within the church body will be fostered by this kind of love-you-good-or-bad commitment.

IMITATION OF CHRIST THROUGH IMITATION WITHIN THE BODY

Several places in the New Testament, Christians are encouraged to imitate other Christians (for example, II Thess. 3:7–9; Heb. 6:12 and 13:7; III John 1:11). In I Corinthians 4:15–17, Paul urges Christians at Corinth to imitate him as he follows Christ. An important way we all learn what it means to be Christian is through imitation of others in the church – again, for better or for worse.

We described earlier the power of automatic and unconscious imitation of others in the development of children and in shaping the behavior and habits of adults. As we learned, imitation is a fundamental process by which the human nervous system comprehends and adapts to the world. We understand the implications of the behavior of others by creating in our brains an action simulation of the behaviors we are observing (as if we were doing the same thing ourselves). Having internally simulated the behavior that we observed and thus having understood it, our nervous system is now primed, increasing the likelihood that we will do the same thing immediately or in a similar situation in the future.

The fundamental imitative character of human nature suggests that all groups of persons – and certainly the church – are characterized by constant, powerful *reciprocal imitation*. I imitate you while you imitate me, and both of us are imitating those around us, who also are imitating us. One need only spend a few hours in a high school or junior high to recognize rampant reciprocal imitation. Group contagion leading to mob behavior is an extreme example. But, however subtle and nuanced they may be, all social interactions involve a complex web of imitative influence.

Of course, we do not all end up doing the same thing. We each have many other agendas and influences that regulate our behavior. However, it can easily be shown in laboratory experiments, as well as in the real world, that we tend to act like those around us – happy or sad, rude or courteous, angry or calm, envious and acquisitive or grateful, quiet or loud, tranquil or excited. Behavior, attitudes, and speech are contagious.

Imitation is too powerful and critical to the formation of our behaviors, habits, and thinking to be ignored in the church. When we as Christians understand our spirituality as merely inside and private, we tend not to notice either the effects of others on our Christian life, or the effects we have on others around us. We tend to think, "My spiritual life is about Jesus and me." Being mostly unaware of these influences, we do not seek to marshal the power of this process, and we miss opportunities to enhance the spiritual formation of one another in the congregation. We also miss, and thus do not take responsibility for, the ways our less-than-holy behavior in the church impacts the formation of fellow congregants.

The role of reciprocal imitation in Christian formation was highlighted in an essay written by eighteenth century German theologian Friedrich Schleiermacher. Schleiermacher was concerned about the problem of how we might learn to be persons whose lives include compassion, particularly habits of benevolence on behalf of the poor.[1] The problem he noted was that neither contemplation of one's own privileged status, nor reflection on one's moral obligations (which often come to mind through teaching and preaching), elicit motivations in us that are sufficient to give rise to a meaningful quality or quantity of compassionate action. The motivational power of pure obligation is insufficient. The solution to this problem for Schleiermacher was through the combination of what has been translated as sociable connections and small-group action. Compared to solo compassionate action, the small-group mode not only has the benefit of being more effective (more people get more accomplished), but the group action simultaneously "strengthens the intensity of the sentiments of those performing the benevolent actions."[2] Within groups of persons engaged together in caring for persons in need, an important new dimension comes into play – the reciprocal imitative strengthening of compassion, with respect to both feelings of empathy and habits of behavior. As theologian Michael Welker describes Schleiermacher's basic idea:

---

[1] Michael Welker, "We Live Deeper Than We Think: The Genius of Schleiermacher's Earliest Ethics," *Theology Today* 56, no. 2 (1999).

[2] Ibid., 173.

"Complex and strengthening sentiments arise in me when my action is embedded in an interconnection with the actions of other human beings."[3] Reciprocal *imitation* is the key factor – we are formed and reformed by observing and imitating one another as we are involved together in the life of God's kingdom and compassionate ministry.

This account is consistent with work done on group psychotherapy by psychotherapist, author, and professor Irvin Yalom described earlier.[4] Two of the eleven primary therapeutic factors in group therapy identified by Yalom are highly consistent with Schleiermacher's perspective – altruism and imitation. As participants observe one another engaging in new ways of interacting, they will tend to try out for themselves similar ways of acting and feeling, including imitation of giving and receiving.

The role of imitation goes beyond things we do. We described earlier the Mimetic Theory of René Girard which proposes that we not only imitate behaviors, but more importantly, we imitate *desire*. According to Girard, all human desire is based on imitation of other persons. Other than basic physical needs, all of our wants and desires come from observing and imitating the desires expressed in the behavior of others. Unfortunately, as Girard points out, when our desire is for an object possessed by the other or for the status of the other, we become envious of this other person and also become his or her rival, either explicitly or implicitly. Therefore, the challenge for the church is to become a place where our imitation of one another results, not in desire for possessions or status, *but in desire for the things of Christ, that is, the desire to love and to serve.* To be sure, what we are saying here so glibly is a huge challenge for any group of persons that desires to become the Body of Christ.

In Chapter 6, we touched on the potential for small groups within the church to bring about significant change in individuals. Jane had the opportunity not only to be shaped by new experiences in her group of believers, but to be in the presence of examples of alternative behaviors and attitudes that she could assimilate by imitation. To become more like Christ, we need examples to imitate. As Schleiermacher suggested, to develop the habits of benevolence, love, and care, we need to participate

---

[3] Ibid., 173.
[4] Irvin Yalom, *The Theory and Practice of Group Psychotherapy*, 3rd ed. (New York: Basic Books, 1985).

with a group in these actions, so that we are able to reinforce in one another such Christlike behaviors and attitudes.

As expressed earlier, the interaction between the power of imitation and the need for the sort of interpersonal attachments that foster openness to growth suggest something important about time and group size. These sorts of interpersonal interactions and relationships are unlikely to develop in large groups or in small groups that are short-term and loosely associated. They are also not apt to lead to significant growth when not active together in significant ministry. For example, Schleiermacher argued that smaller groups – with their more intense sociable connections (or attachments) – afford opportunities for growth through imitation as they are involved in ministry together.

FORMATION THROUGH STORY

Throughout our lives we are guided in our choices and perspectives by implicit stories – for example, stories about being popular, successful, a macho guy, a pretty girl, an athlete, a good parent, a solid citizen, and so forth. Children are often very explicit in their description of what they wish for in their life story, such as "I want to be a scientist when I grow up," or "I'm going to be a baseball player." However, we all have implicit stories that guide our living. We referred to these stories in an earlier chapter as scripts that we carry around in our subconscious minds to use as basic plans for guiding our choices and behavior in various situations.

The stories we live by are never ones that we make up on our own. They are absorbed from those stories told to us by others – parents, mentors, people we admire, teachers, friends, movies or TV shows, and books. As we go through our days, we absorb not only the facts of the situations we encounter, but also the implicit social story line that is being used to frame and characterize the situation. Often it is nothing explicitly said that puts a story into play, but rather the presuppositions behind conversations or the metaphors that are used. One of the reasons language is so powerful and formative is that it functions to put certain implicit narratives into play in various situations.

The church is full of both implicit and explicit stories that shape the individual lives of congregants, as well as the activities and life of the community. For example, "church growth" is a typical congregational story about becoming a larger church through attracting more people to attend services, as well as visions of a larger sanctuary and larger pastoral staff. Another implicit story that sometimes forms the lives of individuals is the health and wealth story, where evidence of financial or professional success is presumed to imply a more admirable Christian life and consequently higher status in the church, whereas those who are poor or physically disabled are not assumed to be of sufficient Christian character to be important in the life of the congregation. Somewhere deep within this "health and wealth" story is a very ancient but un-Christian (pagan) story about poverty or illness being a sign of sin and God's displeasure, whereas health and wealth are a blessing from God, due to the particular spiritual merit of the person. This, of course, was the problem dealt with in the book of Job in the Old Testament. Another example of a story that forms members of a congregation is the narrative about the nature of "spirituality." Although this story is about inward experience, it often tends to focus on certain kinds of public display during worship, ways of talking, or forms of behavioral piety. Such acts may come to form an inclusion-exclusion boundary for who is considered a spiritual person, sometimes even defining who is a "real Christian." If the person doesn't follow the script of the story, the person is not assumed to be a very spiritual Christian.

The Bible is full of stories. These stories are there for us to imitate and incorporate into our lives, such that the biblical story begins to shape our story. The true goal of Christian life is to place our human stories into the larger narrative of scripture in such a way that we become shaped by it. Preaching and teaching are particularly critical in helping our stories – personally and as congregations – to be progressively shaped by biblical narratives. A critical issue in understanding the meaning of the Bible for us is to see how our various stories (such as church growth, health and wealth, spirituality, community, and social gospel) either are or are not compatible with the narrative and teaching of scripture.

We described earlier how comprehension of a story that we hear or read requires action-simulation, such that we mentally simulate the actions we are hearing about in the story and vicariously suffer the good or bad consequences. Thus, stories that we hear or read form us by fostering imitation of actions that in the story led to good outcomes and avoidance of actions with less desirable outcomes. In addition, the stories of scripture can create catastrophe in hearers that push them toward further growth and reformation. Thus, good pastoral theology requires careful, wise, and insightful leading of a congregation into a robust and appropriate incorporation of the stories of the Bible, even though this might create catastrophe.

CHURCH AND THE FORMATION OF PERSONS

In this chapter, we have argued that the central purpose of the church is the formation and growth of Christians. We have also described how formation occurs through participation in and with the Body of Christ – that is, the congregation of Christians that gather in the local church. Finally, we have argued that Christian formation is not ethereal, disembodied, or mystical but is the outcome of interpersonal interactions within the congregation: as we face catastrophes in our lives, as we are loved and supported through times of growth and reformation, as we imitate one another, and as we tell and explicitly or implicitly hear and tell stories that become scripts that guide our lives.

In this chapter, individual Christian formation has been in the foreground, while the church itself has provided the context and background. What needs now to be explored is the nature of a church in which persons are formed and reformed in the image of Christ. It is to this topic that we now turn.

8

~

Church Bodies

IT'S NOT ABOUT ME

I was attending a meeting of the worship committee at the home of our pastor, Josh. We were partway through the Christmas series in our little church and the task of the meeting was to discuss the next series that was going to focus on the mission of the church.

Part of the impetus for the next topic was a comment made by a congregant that he had a hard time describing our church to anyone. Josh was asking us how we talk about our church to those who don't know us. Various comments were made, but we all agreed that we tend to mention our church's founding scripture and consistent challenge, Micah 6:8, "What does the Lord require of you but to do justice, love mercy, and walk humbly with God."

Committee member Sonia then said, "I have to tell you a story. In years past, whenever I have talked about my faith to non-Christians, I was always doing my best to avoid ever mentioning the church. Somehow the church was not only not relevant, but terribly distracting. Last week I spent five hours with a non-Christian friend and we talked a lot about faith. To my own surprise, I found that, having been a part of this church for the past few years, I could not talk about my faith without talking about our church – our community of faith is so much a part of my spiritual life and my faith. It's just not about me or my individual faith."[1]

---

[1] This is a true story narrated by Warren Brown.

CHURCH AND CHRISTIAN LIFE

Sonia's story well captures a major point of this book – robust Christian faith is embedded within and emergent from the life of a community of faith. In the previous chapter we explored the processes of Christian formation and transformation in individual persons, with a particular eye toward our more general discussion of how people develop and change. The strong theme of this previous discussion was the very social nature of all human development. It is primarily in the context of interactions with others that persons change – for better or worse.

Given that the focus of the previous chapter was the Christian formation of individual persons, two questions remain regarding what sort of church fosters adequate Christian formation. First: *How do churches form persons?* Because human formation and transformation are inherently social processes, it is not possible to think about formation of individual persons within a church without also considering the nature of the church itself as a social system or network. Thus, to understand Christian formation, we must consider the church as a system within which individual Christians are embedded, and that the church is itself a body embedded in a wider context – involving both the cultural world and the spiritual environment of the reign of God. How does a church as a dynamical system embody the reign of God, such as to transform both its members and the society within which it is embedded? This leads us to a second related question: *How do groups of individual Christian persons form into a genuine Body of Christ?*

With respect to both questions, the thoughts and ideas we discuss will be in the form of ways to think about these processes, rather than specific things to do or not to do. We cannot provide how-to descriptions for the very reason that what is critical is the form of life of the church body, not necessarily the specific programs or activities. How these perspectives become a part of any particular church body will entail a process of discovery and dynamic transformation of the church itself, much as we have described it in the previous chapter with reference to individual persons.

THE CHURCH AS A DYNAMIC NETWORK

We have described the physical nature of persons using the theory of dynamical systems. Our purpose was to understand persons as embodied, yet more than simply a large mass of cells or organs – that is, a person is a uniquely organized *pattern* that is dynamic in its developmental process of self-organization and in its continual processes of reorganization and transformation in response to new situations and challenges.

Our metaphor for enlightening this process was an ant colony, with the operative parallel being between individual ants within the pattern of activity of the colony as a whole, compared to individual cells of the body or brain within the pattern of activity that represents the person as a whole. Because of the formation of organizational patterns, persons, like ant colonies, come to have ways of interacting with their environments that are characteristic of the individual and adaptive, given the social context and environment. The environmental context provides the initial pressures for adaptive organization in human children, as in young ant colonies. As life progresses, any significant mismatch between the system and the environment (a catastrophe) will trigger a transformation in formation and growth of the organizational pattern that is the person. Currently, the dominant view of families is also to see them as dynamical systems. That is, like the ant colony, a family is more than the sum of its parts, which are the individual family members. A family is not just a group of individuals that come together, but is like a colony or organism where patterns of interactions create roles and tasks for each member. Families, as dynamical systems, also have a collective temperament and even personality. For example, some families are optimistic and openly inclusive of others, while some are pessimistic and closed, and tend to be exclusive of others.

Like all dynamical systems, families strive for sameness, equilibrium, or homeostasis. That is, families strive for a pattern of organization that consistently meets internal needs and external pressures. The organizational pattern that constitutes the family system is an assemblage of long-standing spoken and unspoken rules and family rituals that all members learn and with which they are expected to comply. For example, there are often unspoken rules about what can be said and what should not be said (that is, how much information can pass between members); how boundaries between the family and the world will function (that is, what extrafamily disruptions and changes will be allowed, or what family information can be shared outside the family); and what roles each member of the family will fill, not only obvious roles such as parent and bread winner, but also who in the family disciplines, generates fun, mediates reconciliation, acts out, and so forth. While the size of a family system is small (many fewer individuals than ant colonies), the complexity of human nature makes these organizational patterns variegated and intricate with respect to roles, rules, and rituals.

In our attempt to understand the church, we need to change our viewpoint and recast our ant metaphor from human bodies or families to church bodies. As with families, we can imagine a church as a colony, and the individual members of the congregation as a parallel to individual ants. In all complex aggregations of individuals – whether colonies of ants, troops of chimpanzees, families, or other groups of persons – there is a constant reciprocal interaction of influence between the characteristics of single individuals and the nature of the system as a whole colony, troop, family, or group. The church is a complex system that is more than the aggregate sum of the individuals involved; as in families and ant colonies, this "more than" has a reciprocal transformative impact on the individual members involved.

What is there to be learned about churches when they are understood as dynamical systems? What is the relationship between individual congregants and the life of the congregation as a whole?

BODIES FORMED BY COMMUNICATION

Before attempting to understand the church as a system that is like an ant colony or a family, there is an important presupposition that we need to explore. The reason that a large quantity of individual ants can form and organize into a colony is related to the connectedness and ongoing communication between ants. Airborne interchange of hormone signals called pheromones, as well as physical contact between ants, serve as communication signals that cause individual ants to do one thing versus another. For example, on the basis of such messages, an individual ant might forage for food rather than work on building the structure of the nest or tend the queen. These communications and interactions are what cause large quantities of ants to organize into patterns of activity recognizable as a colony rather than a mere swarm. Colonies do things in the world that individual ants do not do. If you eliminate or reduce communication, a colony does not form, and we have merely an aggregate swarm of randomly scurrying ants.

Similarly, it is close and consistent communications and interactions – whether healthy or unhealthy – that constitute a family as a system. A family is a family based not on biological relatedness or local living arrangements, but on the quality and quantity of communications and interactions. Eliminate communication and "family" ceases to exist.

The same is also true of a church. For the church to be a body – that is, a dynamical system that shapes individuals and has an impact on the surrounding neighborhood and city – there must be sufficient quantity and quality of communication and interaction among congregants. If there is very little or very poor quality interaction and communication, then the church can be no more than a mere collection of persons who happen to swarm at the same place and time in the church building on Sunday morning. In this case, the church is nothing more than a loose association of the independently spiritual. For the church to become an organized body – the Body of Christ – long-term and high-quality interactions need to take place among its members. Ideally, these interactions are characterized by flexibility, adaptability, and interdependence leading to a form of cohesion that is neither rigidly enmeshed nor passively disengaged. A particular church cannot be the *Body* of Christ if it is no more than a loose association of independent Christians, because there is no organized and dynamically interconnected network that could correctly be designated a body. Similarly, the church cannot be a *dynamical* system if relationships and roles are rigid and without flexibility.

RECIPROCAL NATURE OF FORMATION

It is also true of dynamical systems that once a system forms, there is a constant two-way influence between the system as a whole and the individuals that constitute the system. Different species of ants may form different sorts of colonies, given the nature of the individual ants that extend influence to the colony. Even so, a particular ant within a colony is directed and formed to accomplish a certain task, perhaps becoming a forager, by the patterns of interaction inherent in the current organization of the colony; here, the influence extends from colony to individual.

Of course, families are also reciprocal in their influences. The talents and temperaments of each individual feed into the characteristics of the family – influence from individual persons to family – while at the same time families are constituted by different roles for different persons. The interactive patterns within the family define these roles, and the adoption of this role or that role contributes to the formation of each family member – here, influence from family to individual family members. While in ant colonies, roles will shift flexibly depending on internal needs and external threats, it is sometimes the case that families become dysfunctional when roles or role definitions do not change and adapt with changing circumstances, such as the emergence of adolescence in children.

A similar story can be told of the church. The nature of a particular church is to some degree a reflection of the characteristics of the persons who come together to make up this particular church, such that a church made up of urban middle class persons is going to be different in some respects from a church of poor rural farmers, showing influence extending from individuals to church. But if a church really becomes a *body*, the pattern of organization of that body will influence the roles, activities, attitudes, motivations, and lives of its various members. Churches have personalities, that is, describable characteristics of their particular dynamic organization. These personalities are a reciprocal interaction between the characteristics of the individuals in the congregation and the nature and quality of the dynamic organization of the body.

The specific nature of the influences of a church on each individual will be different, depending on the role in the body that the person comes to play. So, if a person's role in a congregation is to help take care of those who are seriously ill, such as visiting in the hospital, taking meals when they return home, and helping interface with medical systems, that role will not only direct and guide the person's activities and efforts within the body, but also progressively form the person; his or her skills, attitudes, and perspectives will be progressively shaped. What is more, the person will be absorbed and integrated into the body of Christ as a member who functions in that particular way to express the compassionate values and attitudes of the entire body.

LEADERSHIP AND SELF-ORGANIZATION

A critical property of dynamical systems is that they are largely self-organizing. In an ant colony, there is no central command system or structure that directs the activities of the individual members, makes whole-system decisions, or distributes labor. What the colony does at any particular moment is determined by the pattern of interactivity through-out all of the ants as they respond to feedback from the extracolony environment (perhaps change in available food supply) and intracolony status (perhaps need for food or nest repair). The amazing thing is that no ant is in charge, making plans, and giving orders – certainly not the queen, which is a very passive egg-layer. All of these complex tasks get done at the right time and in the correct proportion based on the pattern of communication and interaction among thousands of individual ants. Very complex tasks are successfully carried out without any hierarchical command structure. Ants have a few genetically determined behavioral possibilities and a limited range of communication. On the basis of this limited behavioral and communication repertoire, the colony as a whole continually adjusts its patterns of group activity to meet the challenges of changing internal and external environments. Given current needs, varying quantities of ants will be foraging for food, clearing waste from the nest, tending the queen in her egg laying, defending the nest from invaders, or building the nest itself.

Human groups are often similarly self-organizing. Science writer Steven Johnson, in his book on complex systems entitled *Emergence*,[2] describes how the best explanation of the organization and growth of most, if not all, cities is not city planning, which generally comes about somewhat after that fact, but rather the dynamics of a complex self-organizing processes. Cities self-organize physically and socially to meet

[2] Steven Johnson, *Emergence: The Connected Lives of Ants, Brains, Cities and Software* (New York: Schribner, 2001).

internal and external needs. The survival, growth, and thriving of the vast majority of cities gives impressive testimony to the effectiveness of this process. Similarly, while parents often believe they are in charge, such that the family organizes based on their planning, in actuality the family self-organizes via complex interactions among the individuals (their personalities, capacities, and histories) and the ongoing internal and external demands on the family. Changes such as moving to a new neighborhood or the natural maturation of children will trigger a reorganization of the family system quite outside of the conscious dictates of the parents. The new structure arises in a kind of collective unconscious, outside of any one particular member's planning and, as always, for better or worse. Sometimes family life can become difficult or dysfunctional when members of the family do not comprehend the nature of the reorganization and do not have the capacity to adjust to the new demands, perhaps due to the sort of insecurity and interpersonal rigidity we described in Chapter 6.

To the degree that congregations become genuine bodies rather than loose associations of independently spiritual persons, they undergo similar processes of constant self-organization and reorganization, influenced by the characteristics of the congregants, internal and external demands, and the history of the church itself. The patterns of self-organization will also be guided, for better or worse, by dominant themes and stories in the church about the nature of Christian life and ministry. Given sufficient quality and intensity in interactions, adequate feedback regarding the outcome of their work, and a dominant kingdom of God narrative, self-organizing groups of congregants can best meet the internal and external ministry challenges of the church. While patterns of leadership will emerge, directions from the top do not add much to improve this process. Official church leadership roles mostly need to open channels of communication and information feedback about outcomes that will allow continued adjustments and reorganizations of persons and efforts, as well as to tell the stories that bring to mind the nature of the Kingdom of God. In human groups, the processes of self-organization are guided by the dominant narrative – the stories and scripts of the group – as well as ongoing feedback about outcomes. While leadership naturally emerges in human groups, including families and churches, to facilitate group process, the role of leadership should not be overestimated in the face of the power of interactive self-organization of groups with respect to dominant stories, tasks, and environmental demands. Often leadership functions best by telling the story in ways that make apparent the gap between the narrative and ongoing actions, precipitating a sort of catastrophe that forces reorganization.

An important characteristic of complex self-organizing communities like ant colonies, families, and churches is that once the community begins to organize, new properties and capacities emerge that go well beyond what one might predict, knowing the capacities of individual community members. So, in the case of the ant colony, despite the limited behavioral and communication repertoire of individual ants, very sophisticated tasks get accomplished once the colony becomes organized – a nest gets built, food is accumulated to feed the entire community, the queen and her offspring are well tended, garbage gets taken to some distant garbage dump, dead ants are taken to the burial area, and the nest gets defended from the threat of other colonies. None of these tasks would necessarily be attempted by isolated individual ants. These tasks are accomplished because large quantities of ants interact and organize sufficiently to accomplish more sophisticated and large-scale projects. So also, families and churches develop capacities that go well beyond the singular capacities of any of the individuals in the family or church, but emerge from the pattern of organization of the system. When a family *system* or church *body* comes into existence, new capacities emerge to solve problems inside and outside the family or church.

Another important aspect of such dynamical networks is that they are the only really effective means for the spread of formative influence (as opposed to dispersal of information). While information can easily be broadcast to disconnected individuals though preaching and announcements in a church service, influence that is formative of persons spreads through social networks. What is more, the nature of the network has an effect on the strength and spread of influences on particular persons. A recent study was reported on the spread of a particular health behavior through two forms of Internet-based networks. One network was set up with random interconnectivity. Another network was set up with smaller clusters of persons with numerous and redundant interneighbor ties within the cluster, but also with some ties between clusters. It was found that the spread of health-behavior change was much more effective in the clustered network.[3] So, the more a church is a smaller cluster, or includes multiple smaller clusters that also are interconnected with one another, the more likely it is that formative influence, whether healthy or unhealthy, will spread through the entire network. Conversely, large networks – where each person has several randomly distributed connections spread over a larger number of people without identifiable smaller group clusters within which persons are heavily interconnected – are not systems in which formative influences spread effectively.

So, here is the central idea in a nutshell: A genuine church body, as in the Body of Christ, is considerably more than a loose association of independent persons. It is a self-organized interactive network of persons with properties of the whole body that extend far beyond the capacities and characteristics of individual members. And, to the degree that a particular church body has some genuine causal effect on the world around it, the effect emerges primarily out of self-organizing patterns. It becomes a genuine body not by central planning and decisions meted out top-down through organizational hierarchy; rather, what becomes gen-uinely a body is the outcome of self-organizing processes that may (or may not) be happening beneath the official hierarchy. Really effective patterns of organization come about from frequent and close interactions among congregants that are formed and shaped by continual feedback from both internal needs and ongoing action in the world. In addition, it is the experience of being nested within self-organizing and emerging ministry that is reciprocally formative for the persons involved, particularly in clustered networks.

Perhaps this is a time to venture a definition of a "church." A church is a deeply interactive network of Christian persons within which emerges over time properties and patterns that constitute the present and man-ifest Body of Christ, at least in some partially realized form. As such, it becomes a means of grace – a sacrament, if you will – to its own members and to the world. The line of cause in becoming a genuine Body of Christ does not extend *from* the aggregate spirituality of the individual persons that are assembled *to* the church body, but *from* the characteristics that

---

[3] Damon Centola, "The Spread of Behavior in an Online Social Network Experiment," *Science* (Sept. 2010):1194–1197.

emerge in the body as a whole *to* the persons that constitute the body. The direction of influence and cause is mostly from the whole (the characteristics of the church body) to the parts (the Christian character and spiritual life of the individuals). To put it bluntly, a church does not become a genuine Body of Christ by a bunch of Christians becoming "real spiritual," and then getting together in a church. If a genuine body exists, then there is little distinction to be made between the formation of the church as the Body of Christ and the spiritual formation of the members of the congregation. In some sense, the categories of individual and community become blurred, if not indistinguishable.

CHAOS, CATASTROPHE, AND GROWTH

We discussed in earlier chapters the nature of the formation of persons. In doing so, we used the model of complex dynamical systems as a way to understand human beings and their development and growth as persons. Using the language of dynamical systems, we conceptualized the critical force in growth and change as catastrophe. In the language of the dynamical systems model, a catastrophe is said to have occurred whenever the current form of organization of the system does not allow the system to deal effectively with a new context or event. In the face of catastrophe, the system (that is, the person) must reorganize and change. While the overall characteristics of the system are largely the same (for example, the person has a recognizably preserved personality), the organization must shift and reform, to a greater or lesser degree, in order to adequately deal with the new events and situations. This is a basic description of the social and mental maturation of a young child – so many things occur that the child has not previously encountered (frequent catastrophe), and the child must continually adapt to these new experiences in order to learn, grow, and mature.

Similarly, few family systems have become organized in a manner that they are able to deal with a member becoming seriously ill or disabled. This catastrophe (a literal catastrophe in this case) forces a whole-family system adaptation with each member taking on new roles, responsibilities, and relationships. While a lot about the previous forms of family life and organization are preserved, new adjustments are necessary. The family must grow. However, constructive change and growth in such circumstances can only occur when the system is flexible enough to adjust to the new changes. Overly rigid family systems or persons within families have difficulty making such adjustments.

To the degree that a church becomes a body, rather than a loose assembly of individuals, it also grows and matures as it experiences and faces into catastrophe. Like individual persons and families, continuing to grapple with changes and challenges brings about growth and maturity. A church body has a personality and a character that should come to be described by virtues such as wisdom, compassion, hospitality, truthfulness, and holiness. These characteristics arise by flexibly facing new situations and challenges. But sometimes this is not the case. Consider the following story of a fictional church:

Community Church was a medium-sized church that had been in existence for twenty-five years. It began as a "church plant" from a mother church some twenty miles away. It began with a small core group of "planters" and quickly grew in the developing neighborhood in which it was situated. The timing and environment was ripe for a church to grow there and, under the direction of the young pastor and the planting laypeople, it grew over the next seven years to be a church of more than 300.

But then the founding pastor accepted a call to a church out of state, and Community Church was forced to go through a pastoral search. In time they secured a new minister who arrived with new ideas. She noticed that the neighborhood was changing around the church and attempted to create some new programs to reach the evolving demographic. But by this time the lay leadership was deeply entrenched. They didn't like the ideas of the new minister, and it wasn't long before dissention and antagonism grew. Within a couple of years, the new pastor was forced to resign.

A second pastoral search took place, and a third pastor took the helm of Community Church. Surprisingly, this new pastor also found himself at odds with the "powers" of the church, and he too resigned. A fourth pastor emerged only to find herself in a similar situation.

By now an interesting narrative began to emerge regarding Community Church. Most of the congregation bemoaned the fact that they had somehow poorly chosen their past three pastors. At the same time they celebrated that they were able to find a way to "cast them off." Meanwhile, the larger denomination of which Community Church was a part had a different narrative. They viewed the church as controlled by a small but powerful group of laypeople who would not submit to the authority of any pastor. As is the case in most situations where there are two narratives, probably both held some of the truth.

This is a description of a church unable to adapt and grow in the face of catastrophe. Anything that seemed to threaten the status quo or was different from how things had been done in earlier periods when the church seemed to be successful was met with defensive rigidity. For continued growth and maturity, churches need self-definitional stories that embrace change. The body matures through the kind of adjustments and reformations that occur as catastrophes are engaged in the light of the story of the Gospel. If the church is to become the Body of Christ in a real sense, it must continually adapt itself to new situations, but in a way that increasingly manifests the story of scripture about life within the Kingdom of God. In so doing, the church will increasingly come to embody the character of Christ – that is, progressively become a genuine Body of Christ.

Our premise, therefore, is that the force that pushes growth in a church body is the outcome of facing into catastrophe. Meeting the momentary chaos created by new internal and external circumstances in the context of a biblical narrative causes the body to become more and more like Christ. At the expense of dealing in caricature, perhaps this premise would be clearer by stating the alternative point of view. The typical alternative view is that if we can shield the life of the church from any internal and external disturbances and continue our usual form of worship and church programs seamlessly without interruption, distress, or disturbance, members of the congregation will grow as independently spiritual individuals, and perhaps more people will attend as well. This view seeks to isolate the church from encountering any form of catastrophe and to ignore catastrophes when they occur.

With respect to internal catastrophe, the world may "know we are Christians by our love," but not when we ignore or deny conflict and difficulties, or react rigidly to challenges or catastrophes! In fact, it is a powerful witness for those outside to see the church deal successfully, maturely, and lovingly with internal and external disturbances. If, as we believe, the church is a dynamical system, it only grows as it encounters openly and dynamically situations that its current character and form of life are inadequate to meet.

SOURCES OF CATASTROPHE

What sort of events can and should create growth-inducing catastrophe? First, preaching and Bible study should periodically stir up catastrophe. The Word of God should be to a congregation a "two-edged sword" that cleaves not only the life style and values of the world, but also those of the church. It should be a mirror in which our own faces and behaviors are clearly reflected, a window through which we see the needs of people within and without, and a polarizing lens that reduces the glare created by the values "of this present age." If preaching does not, at various times, lead the church into catastrophe and perhaps a period of local chaos, then we would suggest that God's word is not being preached in full. The things that might lead us into catastrophe often are hard to say and harder to hear.

A second experience that can present a church body with catastrophe is the presence of new people who differ from the current congregation with respect to socioeconomic status (perhaps homeless), culture, ethnicity, mental or physical disability, or even sexual orientation. Such persons disturb the status quo and threaten chaos. These are the strangers and foreigners (sojourners) spoken of in scripture. If these individuals are to be able to participate in the church and come to experience the growth as persons that can come from involvement in the interpersonal network that is the church, then the church is usually going to have to reorganize as a system to some greater or lesser degree. But, unfortunately, we often react to the presence of persons who are different by treating them as invisible, implicitly hoping they will go away or, in some tragic cases, asking them to leave the church. New persons who don't exactly fit in should be valued as providing an opportunity for the church to grow as the Body of Christ. After all, Christ was correctly accused of associating with outcasts and sinners.

A third source of growth in catastrophe results from interacting with the surrounding neighborhood. Any attempt at reciprocal hospitality with neighbors, whether individuals, other churches, schools, businesses, and youth programs, are likely to push the church into situations for which its current form of life is not adequate. Being hospitably involved with neighbors will usually demand growth and reformation of the church as a body. We personally have experienced this. We each attend largely Caucasian, mostly English-speaking churches that are periodically involved with a local Hispanic congregation (in one case) and an African American congregation (in another). In both situations, when such culturally different groups get together, it is clear that a certain amount of catastrophe is being faced by both congregations. It is equally clear that both congregations are forced to grow in the process. It is not at all comfortable for any of the groups, but each seems to emerge from the experience having grown into a more genuine and dynamically open Body of Christ.

An unavoidable source of chaos and catastrophe faced by many congregations is major social change, whether local or national. Economic recession cannot be excluded from the life of the church and any attempt to meet the demands and new circumstances it creates forces growth and change. Change in the socioeconomic or ethnic demographics of the city or surrounding community is a catastrophe faced by many congregations, but should be welcomed as opportunity for reformation and growth. Our earlier story of the struggling church attempted to capture the difficulty congregations may have in being open to the growth that can occur in leaning into the challenge of changing neighborhood demographics. A major natural disaster (for example, hurricane Katrina in New Orleans) is a dramatic example of literal chaos and catastrophe faced by some churches that forces major change and growth.

It is a reasonable hope that, for most congregations most of the time, chaos and catastrophe remain constrained and that change can be progressive, so that growth in the Body of Christ can occur without significant distress. However, this is often not the case. Unfortunately, when the forces of catastrophe are too strong and immediate, we naturally react with rigidity and self-preservation. Catastrophe can go either way – into openness to adaptation and growth or into rigidity that vigorously defends the status quo. Whether they are large and dramatic or smaller and progressive, for the Body of Christ to grow, it needs to meet catastrophes with the sort of openness that can foster growth.

GROUP SIZE, GROUP TIME, AND CHRISTIAN FORMATION

In our discussions of personal change and Christian formation (Part II), we emphasized the critical nature of the social environment in shaping development and fostering growth. We described the power of such interpersonal phenomena as imitation, attachment, and language in forming persons. Obviously, these formative social forces work most effectively in relatively small groups of people, involving networks of more strongly linked interpersonal bonds. Thus, there is a relationship between group size and formative influence. Similarly, frequent and consistent time together (group time) is most conducive to formation.[4]

Are there dimensions of group size that are important to consider in imaging the most formative church environment? What size group would allow for sufficiently close interpersonal relationships for the group to be most formative to its members?

British anthropologist Robin Dunbar provided some helpful empirical observations of group size in primate colonies, out of which he proposed what has been referred to as the Dunbar number. Dunbar's research involved observations of the relationship between the maximum size of cohesive groups of primates, as indicated by stable relationships over time, and the size of the brain. He statistically compared the typical size of a stable and flourishing group in thirty-six primate species with the average size of the cerebral cortex of the brain of that species, and found a significant linear relationship, that is, the larger the brain, the larger the typical group. He then extended that relationship to suggest what should be the maximum size of stable and flourishing groups of humans given our brain size. The statistical projection predicted that human groups no larger than 147.8 persons would be able to maintain stable relationships over time – so the Dunbar number was set at 150 persons. As Dunbar wrote, "... there is a cognitive limit to the number of individuals with whom any one person can maintain stable relationships ... [and] this limit is a direct function of relative neocortex size."[5] The implication of

---

[4] The material in this section is taken in part from two previous papers: W. S. Brown and S. D. Marion, "Embodied Persons, Spiritual Formation, and Wesleyan Communities," in T. J. Oord, ed., *Divine Grace and the Created Order: Wesleyan Forays in Science and Theology of Creation* (Eugene, OR: Pickwick Publication, 2009), 198–211; and W. S. Brown, S. D. Marion, and B. Strawn, "Human Relationality, Spiritual Formation, and Wesleyan Communities," in M. K. Armistead, B. Strawn, and R. Wright, eds., *Wesleyan Theology and Social Science: The Dance of Practical Divinity and Discovery* (Tyne: Cambridge Scholars Publishing, 2010), 95–112.

[5] As quoted by Christopher Allen, "The Dunbar Number as a Limit to Group Sizes," Life with Alacrity, www.lifewithalacrity.com/2004/03/thedunbarnumb.html.

the Dunbar number is that human groups exceeding 150 persons have too many people involved for maintaining networks of stable relationships over time.

Obviously, the situation in human life is not that simple. A monkey colony sustains stable relationships based not only on an optimum group size, but also on the benefit of being together at all times. Sustaining stable and significant (that is, reciprocally formative) relationships with everyone in a group of 150 persons would demand considerable time and effort. Anthropologists estimate that for humans to maintain stable relationships with everyone in this size group it would require about 42 percent of one's time spent in the human equivalent of ape social grooming – very close forms of interpersonal contact that form and maintain attached relationships. For this reason, the maximum group size also depends, according to Dunbar, on the degree of social dispersal. Human groups that are dispersed will meet less often, and so the group size will need to be smaller than 150 for sufficient opportunity to form and maintain stable relationships.

The question of stable relationships and group size has also been investigated in the context of social networks as they occur in the cyber space of the Internet (for example, chat rooms, Facebook, and Twitter). The focus here is the capacity of persons to maintain and track ongoing interactions with other people in an interactive Internet-based network. One investigator suggested the following relationships between group size and the level of network meshing:[6]

- The average group size to be able to track others in a totally meshed network (where each person has some direct connection to every other person) is about twelve persons.
- The average size to track others in an optimally meshed network (where each person is at most one or two relational steps away from every other person, and by way of multiple relational paths) is approximately fifty persons.

---

[6] From Ton Zijlstra, "Lurking and Social Networks," Interdependent Thoughts, www.zylstra.org/blog/archives/001183.html.

- The average size to track others in a suboptimally meshed network (where each person is at most a few steps away from any other person, but sometimes via only one relational path) is 150 persons or less.

Thus, we can see that group size determines the level of enmeshment possible. The larger the group, the less completely the members can be connected (enmeshed) with one another. Therefore, the optimal size of any group depends on the level of stable relationships needed or desired for what is to be accomplished. For example, it is known that psychotherapeutic groups are most effective if the group size does not exceed twelve participants – the depth of interpersonal interactions in therapeutic groups needs to be at the level of a very highly enmeshed network for therapeutic change to occur.

The message in this discussion is that the kind of formation and growth of Christian persons that the church desires will demand organization into stable, long-term groups that are smaller than the average church congregation. Different group sizes are going to engender different levels of attachment and reciprocal formation. The typical small group of approximately twelve persons or so will be more enmeshed and, if interactions are of sufficient quantity and quality, in terms of attachments, growth-producing imitation, biblical narratives, and so forth, such groups will be most effective in formation. However, there is a formation-limiting factor of this size of small group due to the minimal amount of diversity that can be achieved. It is natural for such groups to do what is comfortable and to be mutually complicit with the status quo (that is, no growth). Larger groups in the range of fifty persons can have greater diversity in age, socioeconomic level, health and disability status, race, culture, and so forth and thus have greater potential for catalyzing development and formation in its members. However, more time will be necessary for developing stable relationships and robust opportunities for change in a group of fifty than in a group of twelve. Groups exceeding the Dunbar number of approximately 150 are not likely to be formative in significant ways, but may be reasonable for transmitting information, telling the biblical story, affirming belief through sacrament, engendering emotional experiences, and (of course) taking an offering. However, even these events have less impact when they occur in a larger, more loosely connected group.

What we are *not* meaning to imply is that corporate worship in groups larger than 150 persons (or even mega churches) is useless and has no place in Christian life. What we are saying is that we need to understand the very significant limitations of what is possible in a large corporate worship experience and not overestimate its impact. Large corporate worship, where, by necessity, most individuals are spectators, may serve the functions of affirming belief, didactic teaching, telling and retelling the community (biblical) narrative, and at times even creating growth-engendering catastrophes through preaching. What we believe it cannot do is create the kind of imitative, embodied, formational relationships and experiences that are only possible in smaller, more enmeshed groups.

If smaller group size is important, it is also true that frequent and consistent *time* spent in a smaller group is necessary for maximizing the likelihood and the depth of the transformation. This is true both for the persons involved, and for the character of the group itself (the group body). So often Christians assume that a dilettante dabbling into the life of "their church" is spiritually sufficient – participating when it seems interesting and convenient, but not particularly feeling obligated to be a consistent part of the life of the community. However, little of what we have sketched as transformative is possible with minimal and inconsistent involvement of congregants. There will be little attachment, imitation, interpersonal support, storytelling, and the shaping influence of facing catastrophe together.

These issues of group size and group time are why it is important that large churches have "smaller churches" within them, where smaller groups of individuals can, with sufficient time, become more than a loose association of independently spiritual persons, but rather a genuine Body of Christ.

9

∾

The Embodied Church

REINCARNATION OF THE BETHLEHEM MANGER

In the midst of Sonia's story during the worship committee meeting, we were startled by the sound of gun shots coming from just outside the front of the house. We all hit the floor. After calling 911 and waiting to hear the police arrive, we went out to find on the sidewalk next door a young man shot dead and his girlfriend shot in the leg. Apparently the young man, who was part of a gang from another city, had been walking down the street with his girlfriend when he was confronted by members of another gang and shot. We stood amidst the gathering neighbors – all somewhat stunned. For Josh and his family, the rest of the night and much of the next day were filled with police and news media in front of the house and conversations with concerned neighbors.

Such events create incredible fear for everyone living in the neighborhood – certainly also for Josh, who was concerned about the safety of his family, which included his three young boys. Josh decided to do something to deal with the fear descending on his neighborhood. He organized a service on his front lawn for the very next evening.

Getting there late, I ended up standing in the back, leaning on the fence in front of Josh's house. There were thrity to forty persons gathered in the front yard, about half of them Josh's neighbors and about half persons from our congregation who lived close by. Josh was sitting on his front steps and Justin from our church was sitting beside him, playing the guitar as the group sang.

Because it was the Christmas season, the overwhelming impression that kept revolving in my mind was, "Now THIS is a manger scene!"

We had the backdrop of the wood-sided warmth of Josh's small Craftsman home, with the gables outlined by warm, multicolored Christmas lights; all the lights on inside his home and the blinds open, visually inviting us all into the fellowship of his family and signalling openness rather than cloistered fear; candles on the front porch adding the glow that only candles can bring; all of us out on the front lawn like shepherds, sheep, donkeys, and camels gathered at the manger (I did not see anyone I would identify as a wise man); baby Sasha, daughter of Sonia, toddling around (at times at Josh's feet – that part was really cool). It captured my imagination as the perfect reincarnation of the manger in Bethlehem (without the tawdry statues). This is precisely the context in which Jesus comes to dwell. In the midst of fearful circumstances, we heard the message, "Fear not!" In the gathering of the church and the community, he came among the neighborhood, full of grace and truth.[1]

Stories shape the life of groups and congregations, just as they form the character of individual persons. The event described in this story was an outgrowth of a body of Christians who are formed by a different story – a story of God's presence in the midst of distress, anxiety, and threat. The shooting was a tragic event for those directly involved. For most of the neighborhood it elicited the story told regularly on the evening news: "We live in a threatening environment surrounded by risks of harm, and we must protect ourselves – put up a fence, install a home security system, don't go out at night, and be wary of adolescents from certain ethnic or socioeconomic groups." While these measures may or may not be warranted, the basic story is one of threat and self-preservation. But Josh, his neighbors, and a group from the church embodied a different story – the Christmas story of God coming in the midst of threatening and distressing times, and the church's story of openness, neighborliness, and concern for one another. The evening neighborhood service on Josh's front lawn was itself not as critical as the story it told, and which the church and the neighbors performed together that evening.

---

[1] This story is a continuation of the true story beginning Chapter 8 and is narrated by Warren Brown.

CHURCH AS AN ALTERNATIVE NARRATIVE

In the previous section, we discussed the difference between loosely connected aggregates of people and church bodies. We described how *bodies*, in contrast to loose aggregates of persons, are self-forming systems where individual persons are bound together by networks of communication and interaction from which emerge capacities for responding as a whole, both to external situations and internal needs. This dynamic is true for ant colonies, troops of monkeys, and physical human bodies and can be true of human groups, like families and churches. In the case of ant colonies and physical bodies, the communication that allows systems to form is carried by physical signals (pheromones between ants and transmitter molecules between cells). Groups of persons are bound into bodies by a very robust and complex communication system in the form of *language*. We talk, gesture, write, read, telephone, e-mail, text, friend, and tweet. We use language to teach, preach, tell stories and jokes, give opinions, and express emotions. These verbal messages provide a very robust, complex, and highly nuanced form of human interaction that forms us into systems and bodies – or pushes us toward greater isolation.

Words carry implicit and explicit stories gathered from our life experience. Words point to (denote) specific things, actions, or properties that are in some cases physically present, such as "car" denotes a particular form of machine that we drive around that we can at times see, touch, and hear. However, words also carry implicit stories (connotations) mostly formed by the nature and qualities of our previous experience with either the words themselves or the thing to which the words refer. For example (one example in an infinite set of possible examples), the words "human" and "person" largely denote the same physical thing, but "human" has an implicit story about relationships to other species, while "person" carries an implicit story about values and social relationships. As authors we chose one word or the other depending on the sort of background story we intend to imply. For example, in the discussions of this book, we use "person" to imply something that is physical, and yet much more, and that comes into being via relationship.

Very important meanings are also carried in common stories. We discussed in Chapter 4 how stories like Aesop's fables help form the character of children. Story reference continues to be nested within human conversation. The term *sour grapes* is derived from one of Aesop's fables and carries a whole story about our tendency to degrade the value of things we cannot have. To a child who has heard the stories of *Little Red Riding Hood* or *The Three Little Pigs*, the word "wolf" likely carries within it a story about threat. But to the child who has heard or read Native American stories, "wolf" may have a very different connotation about spiritual presence and power. This illustration also helps us understand the power of cultural narratives in shaping a person's perception of the world.

Our choice of words communicates implicit stories. Perhaps you have had this sort of experience. In a faculty meeting, a decision was being discussed. The implicit story in play at the beginning was about academic standards and integrity, and a particular decision was clearly the direction of the meeting. However, about half way through the discussion someone put another vocabulary (and thus another story) into play regarding compassion for the difficulties of this individual's circumstances. This new story began to reverse the direction of the discussion toward a completely opposite outcome. Two different implicit stories drove the group in entirely different directions with respect to the final decision. Each implied story led to different actions and consequences.

Stories, whether explicitly told or implicit in the semantics of the words that are chosen, are important forces in the formation of bodies of persons in a number of ways. First, stories cause us to *consider actions and their consequences*. This is true because they are understood by mental simulation. To understand the action in a story, we use our systems for controlling our own action to mentally simulate the actions described in the story, but without actually moving ourselves. So, stories force us to act (implicitly) and to comprehend the consequences of the actions as told in the story. To understand the story of the Good Samaritan is to find ourselves in the roles of the various characters, mentally doing the actions that the story describes and observing their impact on other characters in the story. We also attune our emotions to those of the victim and the Samaritan. When this story is told in a church, feelings are engaged about the plight of other persons and action tendencies are engaged for the provision of help and care. Of course, stories can also incline a congregation in the wrong direction, such as implicit or explicit stories implying that wealth is an index of God's particular blessing.

Of course, the action consequences of a story are modulated by the social location and social history of the listeners. Groups in different cultures will hear the same story differently depending on the formational history of the persons and group. In a quasi-experimental study, New Testament professor Mark Alan Powell [2] had seminary students read the story of the Prodigal Son (Luke 15:11–32) and then recount the story to a partner. Out of a hundred American students, only six mentioned the famine that is in Luke's tale. When Powell conducted the same experiment with Russian students in St. Petersburg, forty-two of fifty students mentioned the famine. This cultural focus makes sense given the 1941 German siege of St. Petersburg that led to a 900-day famine in which 670,000 people died of starvation. The traumatic event is still a part of the collective memory of residents of St. Petersburg.

Not only does social location cause individuals to give emphasis to a different part of a story, but it also may lead to hearing very different stories. For the Americans, the sin of the story (that is, what the son did wrong) was the son squandering his money. For the Russians, the sin was the son wanting to be self-sufficient. When Powell repeated this same process with a group of African students in Tanzania, he asked them, "Why does the young man end up starving in the pigpen?" They didn't respond as the Americans ("He wasted his money."), nor as Russians ("There was a famine."). Eighty percent of Tanzanian students responded, "Because no one gave him anything to eat."

Second, *stories construct identity.* A body of persons understands itself in the context of a narrative involving the past and future, relationships with the surrounding world, and relationships within the group. Group narratives answer both the identity question, "Who are we?" and questions about the group's telos, "Where are we going, and what is our purpose?" Thus, the narrative shapes the mission, values, practices, and ethics of the group. For example, there are identity telos stories about what it means to be a corporation, small business, school, entertainment medium, charitable organization, medical clinic, sports team, rock band,

---

[2]   Mark Alan Powell, *What Do They Hear? Bridging the Gap between Pulpit and Pew* (Nashville: Abingdon, 2007).

or street gang. The church has (should have) a self-identity and telos story about what it means to be a local, current embodiment of Christ and the Kingdom of God. However, other stories dominant in the surrounding culture frequently overwhelm this story, shaping the church in ways it does not intend. For example, it is all too easy for churches to come to respond primarily to a corporate, entertainment, charity, psychotherapeutic, or consumerist sort of institutional story. Max DePree, a past president of Herman Miller, Inc., writes about stories in institutions, "Every family, every college, every corporation, every institution needs tribal storytellers. The penalty for failing to listen is to lose one's historical context, one's binding values."[3]

Third, *stories make the world comprehensible and meaningful.* They set the relevant vocabularies and categories, establish values, determine perception (what is seen and what is not seen in a situation), and determine the identity of critical characters in life. Stories are necessary for our thinking because there is usually a vast array of important elements in the situations that we must comprehend. The critical information in most situations is far too complex and variegated to be held in our mental systems as a mass of simultaneous discreet elements of thought or memory. However, stories assemble into a comprehensible, organized, and meaningful package a vast array of particulars that are otherwise many orders of magnitude too many and too complex to be processed by the mind all at one time. The common adage, "not able to see the forest for the trees," points to this problem in understanding, thinking, and problem solving. Without being able to see an organizing pattern (or story) that might make things comprehensible and guide action, we are simply flooded by a whole lot of disorganized particulars.

A church's story allows it to understand itself, as well as the meaning of the variety of lives, histories, personalities, and abilities of the members of the congregation. The story also illuminates the nature of the very complex culture in which the church exists. The church should tell and embody a core story about the Kingdom of God that gives it a basis for understanding the nature of its communal life, as well as shedding light on a host of important cultural issues, such as wealth, power, politics, economics, war and international conflict, consumerism, individual

---

[3]   Max DePree, *Leadership is an Art* (New York: Dell Publishing, 1989), 82.

rights and responsibilities, poverty and homelessness, sports and entertainment, marriage and family, neighborhoods, cities, and much more.

And finally, and perhaps most importantly, *stories regulate imagination*
with respect to what is possible – what is likely to happen, what can and
should be accomplished, and what might be the most meaningful and
Christian thing to do. The story that governs the life of the church
determines whether one thing or another can be imagined as a reasonable
or worthy possibility for the life and activity of the body. Imagination shifts
in a dynamic manner as different stories are made relevant. Thus, we
sometimes imagine different possibilities by altering the story in play. For
example, a group of church leaders might be making plans (imagining
possible actions and outcomes) regulated largely by a corporate story
(success, growth, financial stability), when a member makes a comment
that implies the Kingdom story of "good news to the poor," causing the
imagination of the group to shift to a different domain of possibilities.
Different stories embody different actions and consequences, and putting a
different story into play will influence action.

A very good resource for understanding the importance of narrative to
the life of the church is provided by theologian Stanley Hauerwas in his
essay on Richard Adams's book *Watership Down*. Adams's novel is a
political fantasy about the heroic adventures of a group of rabbits who set
out in search of a new warren.[4] As Hauerwas describes it, the various
communities of rabbits in this novel are "judged primarily by their ability
to sustain the narratives that define the very nature of man, or in this case
rabbits."[5] According to Hauerwas, in flourishing communities, stories
are formative in defining the adventure that the group pursues. "[T]he
basic task of any polity is to offer its people a sense of participation in an
adventure. For finally what we seek is not power, or security, or equality,
or even dignity, but a sense of worth gained from participation and
contribution to a common adventure."[6] In the church, Hauerwas argues,
narratives should provide structures of Christian convictions and ethics
for the life and adventure that the church pursues.

---

[4] Stanley Hauerwas, *"A Story-Formed Community: Reflections on Watership Down,"* in
Stanley Hauerwas, *A Community of Character: Toward a Constructive Christian Social
Ethic* (University of Notre Dame Press, 1981), 9–35.
[5] Ibid., 12.
[6] Ibid., 13.

The pursuit of a story-formed adventure also provides the context and virtues that allow the unexpected to be accepted as a gift – that is, another meaningful event in the saga.Therefore, stories need to be open, dynamic,and adventuresome in the minds of church members, allowing the story to shift or new stories to be adopted as circumstances change. Groups, organizations, or congregations can develop a local culture that clings tenaciously to a rigid story, such as "Things must go according to this plan!" or "There is no other explanation for what we are experiencing!" Such rigidity severely limits the ability to imagine a range of possibilities.

EMBODIED WORSHIP

Worship involves expressing our devotion to God. Thus, it includes not only corporate worship, but potentially all aspects of our lives if lived in such devotion. Corporate worship, our primary topic in this section, is the gathering of the church for the specific intent of engaging in group practices and expressions of devotion. Even in this context, the meaning of the term "worship" is sometimes limited to times of praise singing sandwiched around prayers, but we mean to include as worship all elements of a corporate worship service (preaching/teaching, Eucharist, scripture reading, and even the body life expressed in announcements).

What should be the nature of worship if those who are gathered are physically embodied persons rather than souls occupying bodies? We believe that worship that is truly embodied must form the body as opposed to being solely experiential. Corporate worship is a critical part of the formation of both individual Christians and the church itself. Thus, it is important to consider it more deeply, keeping the embodiment and social embeddedness of persons clearly in view. If we are bodies, then what is *done* – as opposed to simply what is *said* or *experienced* – has greater importance and demands greater intentionality.

Worship traditions and styles come in such great variety that it is difficult to outline or prescribe the particulars of a form of worship that would be most consistent with this view of human nature. Any attempt to be overly specific would probably be useful to only a very few readers, but might be seen by many others as incompatible with their worship tradition. The patterns and practices of specific churches are influenced not only by their denominational tradition, but also by their particular settings and self-definitional stories. However, it is possible to consider some general implications and principles of embodied worship, leaving our readers to think through what these concepts and ideas might imply for their particular worship tradition.

Most generally, for worship to be robustly formative of individuals and the church, care must be taken to ensure that worship does not *disembody* either the individuals participating or the church itself, and that it does not disconnect worship from the daily life of the church and its members.

First, to disembody *individuals* is to engage in worship in such a way that it focuses the attention of congregants inward to their own individual experience, as if spirituality is inside. An inward focus assumes the existence of a self, or mind, or soul inside that is different from who and what we are as whole persons, sitting in a worship service among other Christians. It also assumes that God is inside, rather than present in the room and outside of (other than) any individual. It is not that we do not have the experience of thinking in the form of a seemingly inner dialogue (for example, prayer that we formulate in our consciousness, but that is not verbalized). However, such silent thought and prayer is not the activity of a separate inner being or directed toward an inner presence, but is the response of the whole physical person directed outward to God, but operating off-line. The goal of worship is not to cultivate something inside, but, in unison with those gathered, to worship God who is outside of us as individuals, yet *present between us* – in our midst. We do not gather in order for each individual to have some kind of inner experience or feeling, but for each person and the gathered church to be formed through the context of worship. Focus outward also allows worship to include the formative interpersonal forces we have described, such as attachment, imitation, shared attention, empathy, and life-shaping narrative.

The issue of feelings and emotions in worship is perhaps worth further comment. Emotions are continuous brain-body adjustments and attunements to our current situation, most particularly our social situation. When they become more intense, we say we "have" a particular emotion (fear, joy, sadness), but in reality they are constant processes by which our bodies adjust to the circumstances. In this respect, emotions are never entirely our own, but are things that occur as we encounter one another – sometimes attuning ourselves to each other and sometimes

confronting each other. Therefore, emotions in worship are not manifestations of an inner separate part (the soul) that is independent and
disconnected from the social (communal) environment of worship. They
are by-products of automatic bodily adjustments to the situation that,
when experienced consciously, provide information about the nature of
our current relationship to the social surrounding. So, of course, emotions will always come along with worship, in that they are an important
part our social embeddedness. But, it is also true that, being indices of our
social situation, they are easily manufactured and manipulated.
Therefore, we always need to be careful of the interpretation of our
emotions, not only in experiencing the emotion, but in evaluating its
source – even in worship.

Second, worship can facilitate or hinder the formation of the *church as
a body*. The issue of worship that threatens to disembody the church is
whether it causes individuals to become more and more autonomous and
isolated (focusing on inward thoughts, experiences, and feelings), allowing the church itself to be nothing more than a loose association of
independently spiritual persons. The alternative is worship that more
deeply and meaningfully interconnects the lives of those present, and
thus *forms* the church increasingly into a legitimate body – the Body of
Christ. The more persons sit passively and view the program at a
distance, or become focused inwardly such that those around them
cease to exist in their consciousness, the more worship serves to disembody and disintegrate the Body. The result is worship that is about "Jesus
and me," rather than "Jesus and we." Genuine church bodies emerge
from connectedness, interaction, sharing, communication, corporate
prayer, and common story. To foster autonomous worship (despite
being together in an auditorium or sanctuary) that does little to encourage deeper and more meaningful connectedness between those attending, is to disembody the church.

Third, both individuals and the church become disembodied when
worship is not seen as part of the ongoing daily life of the church and
the lives of each member. If worship is viewed as more spiritual than the
rest of life, then worship has become a mystical Gnostic rite, rather than
an expression of the entire life of the congregation. When certain music
is played, candles lit, liturgy recited, the Bible read aloud, and the
preacher speaks, God is not more present than when we gather in the

vestibule, have a meal together, give our time and effort to works of compassion, or go to work each day. To make it appear so is to make the experience of worship disconnected and disembodied for members of the congregation. Corporate worship is necessary for vital Christian life, but it is not sufficient unto itself. It must be seamlessly continuous with the rest of the daily communal life of the Body of Christ. It is the totality of ongoing life that constitutes worship. "Therefore, I urge you bothers and sisters, in view of God's mercy, to offer your bodies as a living sacrifice, holy and pleasing to God – this is your true and proper worship" (Romans 12:1, NIV).

At the expense of coming too close to specific traditions and styles of worship, we venture a few comments on several specific parts of worship – liturgy, Eucharist, and music – in order to make clearer and more practical the general principles mentioned above. Liturgy is an important part of all worship traditions. Although the term is sometimes associated with High Church traditions, it exists just as certainly in Low Church traditions. Liturgy literally means "the work of the people," and thus refers to the patterns and rituals that all churches engage in on a regular basis. However, the aspects of liturgy we want to emphasize as most conducive to embodied worship are those that are most active, participative, and interpersonal. Corporate worship is most clearly about persons as bodies and active agents when we are engaged together in common activity – when, for example, we read responsively scriptures or texts, pray aloud, sing congregationally, or celebrate the Lord's Supper. The overall structure of liturgy (that is, gathering for and giving voice to praise, hearing God's word, responding in faith, sending forth) should not be merely sections in the program for each Sunday service, but should designate what people actually *do* during various parts of a worship service. When they are participatory events, these categories of liturgy function to form persons and the church into the image and likeness of Christ – to make the church the Body of Christ. When liturgy is done well, and again this may vary in different traditions, worship becomes a fully embodied and communal event that encourages participation and engages all of the person. However, even very participative worship can become problematic when understood and practiced in two polar opposite ways: (1) if forms of participation come to be viewed as a spiritual rites that qualify persons as Christians in some mystical manner;

or (2) if participative liturgy is understood only as a means of fostering agreement with certain statements of belief.

Eucharist is a part of the worship life of most congregations. It is particularly noteworthy within this conversation as a form of embodied corporate worship, because it functions most explicitly as a physical practice of both individuals and the church. First, participation in the Lord's Supper is a very physiological thing to do – one eats and drinks in remembrance of Christ's last earthly meal. Second, it is inherently participatory and active – it is difficult to imagine vicarious participation that would have any real meaning. Third, the symbolic meaning of the ritual is very much about the embodied suffering, death, and resurrection of Jesus. Eucharist is often framed as relevant not only to our sin, but also our suffering. Finally, we take the elements together as the church – it is a communal act, with all the power of reciprocal imitation that contributes to the formation and integration of the congregation into a genuine body. From this perspective, Eucharist seems to us to be most clearly a form of embodied worship in cases where the congregation is invited to go forward to receive the bread and wine (we must respond together more actively – get up, walk, perhaps kneel).

Another part of worship frequently discussed is music. Here again there are many styles and traditions. Like liturgy, music should be participative in a way that embodies both the individual congregant and the church as a whole. For example, because music is inherently emotional, congregational singing tends to create emotional attunement with one another and a strong sense of togetherness. However, some of the value of this interpersonal attunement can be lost if singing is not experienced as together and corporate – that is, when members cannot hear each other, but hear only the leaders and accompaniment. Attention must be also paid to the meaning of the poetry. Some lyrics serve to foster an inward focus and/or presume an autonomous and individualist form of spirituality For example, consider the lyrics of the old hymn, "In the Garden": "I come to the garden alone . . . and he walks with me and talks with me."

Musical performances by soloists or smaller groups in worship, while they can be experienced as an offering of one or several persons to the rest of the church body and to God, may also create a sense of passivity among those listening or engender an entertainment sort of disconnectedness and distance from those performing. We may be entertained or emotionally moved, but possibly not actively engaged or connected to one another. If the objective of worship is formation rather than experience, then criteria for decisions about music in worship will change.

In this section on embodied worship, we have been arguing for the importance of participative action in the engagement of worship – such as a more active liturgy, singing that binds the congregation, and participation in the Eucharist. Our reason for this emphasis is our view of human nature and the attempt to move away from concepts of non-material inner individualist events as constituting formative worship. What we think and experience during worship, is what our bodies are doing. So, to attend to bodily activity in worship is to be explicitly conscious of how the congregation is being formed in Christian faith, wisdom, and character.

Remember, it is not just that what is thought or experienced occurs in the brain and is expressed in the body, but the impact goes the other direction as well: *actions influence thought.*[7] As we described in Chapter 5, what we do with our bodies has a profound influence on what we think. Recall how children who are encouraged to gesture along with a lesson learned more and were better able to solve similar problems on their own. Thus, to participate in the Eucharist during worship (an extended form of gesture) is for this bodily activity to have a deep influence on our thoughts, feelings, beliefs, and future behavior quite beyond what is said. So, our argument for the role of participation and action in worship is an argument based on the profound embodiment of all thought. Without concurrent action, thought and belief is likely to degenerate into nothing but intellectualism, and worship into mere feelings. Formation of persons will be minimal.

We mentioned earlier the issue of group size. It is certainly easier for worship to be an expression of the physically embodied and socially embedded nature of persons when there are a smaller number of persons participating. It is easier to be both participative and interconnected in meaningful ways with a smaller group of individuals. Therefore, for larger churches, this again suggests the importance of smaller groups that gather regularly for body life, including some aspects of corporate worship and active ministry.

[7]   Susan Goldin-Meadow and Sian L. Beilock (2010) op cit.

DISABILITY, DEPENDENCE, CHRISTIAN FORMATION, AND FLOURISHING

Much of what we have been discussing regarding the implications of the physical nature of Christian life and community comes into sharp focus in the context of illness and disability.[8] When the real person is understood as inside and nonmaterial (that is, a soul), it becomes difficult in a religious community to take illness and disability as seriously as it should be taken. The story we inhabit is dominated by the idea that if it is "well with the person's soul" then the plight of the body does not need to occupy as much of our attention and does not carry the same obligation for us to respond with care. But the situation is very different in a worshipping community of persons whose narrative is formed by a view of themselves as physical bodies.

Philosopher Alasdair MacIntyre has provided an important resource for thinking about disability and disease in his book *Dependent Rational Animals*[9] (mentioned also in Chapter 5). For MacIntyre, the goal of human development is to become an "independent practical reasoner," and it is this capacity that allows a person to contribute to the flourishing of others. As you may remember, the critical step in becoming an independent practical reasoner is development of the virtue of "acknowledged dependence." It is a fundamental paradox that only those persons who are continually able to deeply acknowledge, and function within, their dependence on others are successful in becoming truly effective independent practical reasoners, with the wisdom and virtue sufficient to contribute to the well-being of others and the community.

An important domain in which acknowledged dependence and practical reasoning is necessary, particularly within the church, is the response to illness and disability. MacIntyre makes two important points about disability. First, he points out that we are *all always* somewhere on a continuum of disability. He writes, ". . . there is a scale of disability on which we all find ourselves. Disability is a matter of more or less, both in

---

[8] This section is taken in part from Warren S. Brown, "Human Nature, Physicalism, Spirituality, and Healing: Theological Views of a Neuroscientist" *Ex Auditu* 21 (2005):112–127.

[9] Alasdair MacIntyre, *Dependent Rational Animals: Why Human Beings Need the Virtues* (Chicago: Open Court, 1999).

respect to degree of disability and in respect of the time periods in which we are disabled."[10] There is no such thing as a dichotomy between persons who are disabled and those who are not disabled. We all simply reside for the moment at some place along a continuous scale of disability. Throughout our lives, from infancy to old age, we move back and forth along this scale. Thus, for MacIntyre, part of becoming an independent practical reasoner is being clear about our own personal involvement in disability. Identifying ourselves as a part of the disability scene is an important part of acknowledging our dependence.

Second, MacIntyre argues that the flourishing of persons with disability (which includes us all) is dependent on the imaginative and creative involvement of the surrounding community, particularly those who have well developed capacities as practical reasoners. MacIntyre writes,

For it is and perhaps always has been a common assumption that blindness, deafness, deformed or injured limbs, and the like exclude the sufferer from more than a very, very limited set of possibilities. And this has often been treated as if it were a fact of nature. What is thereby obscured is the extent to which whether and how far the obstacles presented by those afflictions can be overcome or circumvented depends not only on the resources of the disabled – and these will vary a great deal from individual to individual – but also on what others contribute, others whose failures may be failures of imagination with respect to future possibilities. What disability amounts to, that is, depends not just on the disabled individual, but on the groups of which that individual is a member.[11]

Thus, MacIntyre believes that the ultimate outcome of a situation of disability – the degree to which a more disabled person can yet flourish – is critically involved with the ability of the immediate community to imagine future possibilities, and to put that imaginative thinking into operation on behalf of the disabled person.

So, what does the concept of spiritual formation mean for those who suffer greater disability? Is it primarily related to the well-being of an inner part (the inner self or soul), or does their flourishing depend upon imaginative actions by, and interactions with, the communities in which disabled persons find themselves? Is it a *spiritual* transformation of the *disabled* and suffering

---

[10] Ibid., 73.
[11] Ibid., 75.

person that is most needed, or is it an *embodied* transformation within *those who immediately surround* the disabled person – a transformation toward the acknowledgement of their own dependence, and a transformation evidenced in engagement of the practical reasoning of the members of the community in imagining solutions to the limitations of disability?

It is too easy in our Gnostic spirituality to relegate Christian solutions to issues of illness and disability to the realm of the inner subjective experiences of the self or the soul, and to ignore the embodied realities of disability and what might be done to minimize these limitations. We easily relegate the needed formation and transformation to the immateriality of the soul of that disabled person, at the expense of the acknowledgement of our own dependence and its implication for what we might be called upon to imagine and do for those who currently suffer greater disability.

Imaginating transformative responses extends even to the flourishing of those with severe cognitive disability (whether congenital in a disorder like Down's syndrome, acquired by brain disease or injury, or due to a progressive dementia like Alzheimer's disease). Because of their disability, persons with the cognitive disability cannot offer an equal contribution to interpersonal relationships, which are a core aspect of personhood. Therefore others will need to contribute more to sustaining and fostering relatedness. In this sense, the relationship is asymmetric.

In fact, the ideal of equal contribution to moments of interpersonal relatedness is often unmet in social relationships. In engaging in relationships, we are at times able to contribute more than our share, but at other times we are constrained by ability or circumstances to a lesser contribution. Thus, the social imagination necessary to foster adequate interpersonal relatedness in those who are cognitively disabled is not a special case. We all move back and forth along the "scale of disability on which we all find ourselves"[12] and, thus, there is an inescapable dynamic of fluctuating contribution that is part and parcel of human life. The fact that we are regularly called upon to contribute more than an equal share to sustaining relatedness with other persons, particularly persons with

---

[12] Ibid., 73.

lesser capacity, forms a critical core of the vocation of Christian living.[13]

All that has been said above about physical or cognitive disability can be broadened to include individuals struggling with psychological disorders (such as those experienced by Jane in Chapter 6), as well as those dealing with substance abuse and various addictions. Although different in some ways to those with physical disability, psychological disorders also move us along the continuum of disability and dependence. While the church has too frequently treated individuals dealing with addictions with disembodied spiritual interventions – for example, the simple but seldom effectual formula, "Repent, and go and sin no more" – what they truly need is the engagement of the community's imagination regarding possibilities for embodied action and support in their recovery. The church's neglect of its responsibility to the whole person, including the physical, cognitive, and psychological, may help explain why psychotherapy and support groups such as Alcohol Anonymous have flourished outside the church. Thankfully, we are seeing an increasing acknowledgment of the role of the church in this kind of restoration process, including the development of church-based programs such as Celebrate Recovery, an explicitly Christian twelve-step program for recovery and in-house church counselling programs.

Some will inevitably ask, "Can't a person maintain a dualist perspective on the human person and still care for persons who are sick or disabled?" To this we would say, "Yes, but ..." While one may care for the body-part of a body-soul duality, the motivation and understanding for *why* to do so is very different. From the point of view of embodied persons, the "why we care for bodies" is because persons *are* bodies. When the church cares for human bodies – when it disciples them, baptizes them, feeds them, clothes them, visits them in prison – it is doing these things to and for the whole person, because bodies are what

[13] With respect to asymmetric relatedness, see W. S. Brown, "Cognitive Contributions to Soul," in W. S. Brown, N. Murphy and N. H. Malony, eds., *Whatever Happened to the Soul? Scientific and Theological Portraits of Human Nature* (Minneapolis: Fortress Press, 1998); W. S. Brown, "Nonreductive Physicalism and Soul: Finding Resonance between Theology and Neuroscience," *American Behavioral Scientist* 45 (2002):1812–1821; and W.S. Brown, "Neurobiological Embodiment of Spirituality and Soul," in Malcolm A. Jeeves, ed., *From Cells to Souls – And Beyond: Changing Portraits of Human Nature* (Grand Rapids: Eerdmans, 2004), 58–76.

we are! When a dualist does these same things, there remains the subtle (sometimes not so subtle) implication that these body things are a *means to an end*. What is most important to the dualist is that something "inside" changes, and caring for the body facilitates that process. A hierarchy remains – soul good, body not so good. And within this hierarchy, it is easier to denigrate the body and all things bodily.

THE PHYSICAL LIFE OF THE CHURCH

For the members of a particular church to form into a body – a dynamical system that acts Christianly in the world – it must have an organizing and action-guiding narrative. Physical human bodies organize around the goal (telos) of homeostasis, and personhood organizes within social relationships around challenges involving self-identity, self-within-family, peer relationships, personal effectiveness, aspirations, and so forth. Bodies of persons, including families and churches, organize around group-encompassing stories about group identity, social relationships, goals, and ideas of success. The story around which the group understands and organizes itself determines both internal relationships (roles and kinds of interactions) and its action in the world. A church body becomes the Body of Christ when the biblical story comes to narrate all of the different sorts of internal interpersonal relations and its missional engagement with the world.

The life of a church in worship is critical for its development into a genuine body rather than a loose association of independently spiritual persons, as well as the formation of the church body and the persons attending into the likeness of Christ. Therefore we argued that the goal of worship is primarily formation rather than experience. Thus, an important principle of worship is to avoid disembodying persons or the church itself through a worship process that focuses persons on themselves (their inward and independent soul), disintegrating the connectedness that would allow the church to become a genuine body.

Finally, disability is a context in which the embodiment of personhood must be kept foremost in our minds. If persons are indeed bodies, then the ethical call and vocation of the church to actively, compassionately, and imaginatively care for persons with disabilities of all kinds comes into clear focus.

Concluding Thoughts: The Church After Dualism

EMBODIED FOREGIVENESS

A few days later, when Jesus again entered Capernaum, the people heard that he had come home. They gathered in such large numbers that there was no room left, not even outside the door, and he preached the word to them. Some men came, bringing to him a paralyzed man, carried by four of them. Since they could not get him to Jesus because of the crowd, they made an opening in the roof above Jesus by digging through it and then lowered the mat the man was lying on. When Jesus saw their faith, he said to the paralyzed man, "Son, your sins are forgiven."

Now some teachers of the law were sitting there, thinking to themselves, "Why does this fellow talk like that? He's blaspheming? Who can forgive sins but God alone?"

Immediately Jesus knew in his spirit that this was what they were thinking in their hearts, and he said to them, "Why are you thinking these things? Which is easier: to say to this paralyzed man, 'Your sins are forgiven,' or to say, 'Get up, take your mat and walk'? But I want you to know that the Son of Man has authority on earth to forgive sins." So he said to the man, "I tell you, get up, take your mat and go home." He got up, took his mat and walked out in full view of them all. This amazed everyone and they praised God, saying, "We have never seen anything like this?" [Mark 2:1–12, NIV]

This book has been about bodies – human bodies and church bodies. Our premise has been that viewing persons as bodies, not souls inhabiting bodies, is truer to scripture, as well as more resonant with modern neuroscience and psychology. Most Christians believe that humans are souls that *have* bodies, not that we *are* bodies. They presume that the "real me" is not their body or even their behavior, but is something inside them, in their head or heart – in their mind or soul. Thus, it is possible to be spiritual inside, without being religious in what we do – without participating in the communal religious life of the church. However, Christian life has a very different feel if the essence of a human person is not a ghostly, immaterial soul or spirit that is temporarily trapped in a fleshy body and hidden from view, but is the indivisible composite of the behavior, habits, thoughts, emotions, and personality of the physical body itself. In this book, we have tried to show how this view: (1) provides a richer perspective on how we become Christian persons, and (2) bestows a more vital role for the life of the church.

Thus, we have been exploring the implications of the embodied and socially embedded nature of persons. As we have described, the state of knowledge in psychology and neuroscience suggests the importance of processes of developmental openness and self-organization, attachment, imitation, and stories in the development of persons. This knowledge provides a different perspective and sets new priorities for understanding conversion, fostering the formation of Christian persons, and, as churches, becoming genuine Bodies of Christ. Whereas the current view of Christian life, as care for the status of souls, focuses on inwardness and individuality, care of embodied persons is fundamentally physical, social, and communal.

The passage from the Gospel of Mark that begins this chapter is a wonderful example of care for embodied persons that is altogether physical, social, and communal. When there was literally no room in which to get the paralyzed man to Jesus, his friends dug a hole in the roof and lowered the man down to Jesus. Mark writes that when Jesus saw *their* faith, he forgave the man's sins, and, in the same act, healed him. Jesus' response was about the whole person. He made little distinction between forgiving sin and healing the man's paralysis. In addition, it was the collective faith and action of the paralyzed man and his friends that led to his restoration and healing. This was not an individualized personal faith, but a communal one! What is more, as a healed and whole person, he no longer carried the community stigma that he was crippled because of some sin committed by him or his family (see John 9:1–5).

With this stigma lifted, and his illness (impurity) gone, he could now enter the temple and worship freely. He was restored to community. It was salvation, healing, and social redemption – altogether.

REVIEW OF PART III

The final section of this book, Part III, contains our primary message. In this section, we took the view of human nature as physical and embodied (as described in Part I) and the implications of this view for the development of persons (dealt with in Part II), and used them to create a renewed understanding of the life of the church and its role in both transformation of persons and engagement in mission. So much of contemporary congregational life, worship, and ministry are rooted in a distinction between body and soul. So, the question we attempted to answer in Part III was, "What should churches be like if persons are inherently physically embodied and socially embedded?"

Chapter 7 attempted to answer this question with respect to the Christian formation of individual persons. Critical to our perspective was the understanding of persons as open and self-organizing systems that are formed as they interact with the social networks within which they are embedded. Therefore, the relational network that constitutes a particular church should be or become the sort of network in which persons are progressively formed into the likeness of Christ. Such growth of persons is dependent on significant depth and quality of interpersonal interaction and interdependence. The characteristics of relationships that are particularly conducive to formation that we discussed were secure attachments, reciprocal imitation, and community storytelling. Persons become more and more Christian as they are nested within an accepting and loving group of persons who imitate one another, as each and all attempt to imitate Christ, and who tell and live into a biblical narrative of life.

In Chapter 8 we dealt with the church itself as a literal *Body* of Christ. We described the church as a dynamical system similar to biological organisms, ant colonies, individual persons, and families. The church becomes a genuine *body* (a dynamical system) to the degree that it is a closely interactive network of individuals. When it has become such a body, the church is situated to be dynamically and progressively formed, both through its communal life of worship and continued probing of scripture, and by its attempts to meet challenges in its internal and external circumstances (catastrophes). Since the embodiment of the church is dependent on the strength of its relational network, there are implications to be considered with respect to group size and the amount of time spent in life together. It is only in the characteristics of its nature as a genuine body that the church can have an impact on the world.

Finally, Chapter 9 looked at several more specific aspects of the life of the church. First, a church body will be a Body of *Christ* depending on whether the story of scripture comes to narrate the life of the church – a story that is markedly different from that of the surrounding culture. Since worship forms the central focus of the weekly life of the church, we also discussed the ways in which worship can either facilitate or hinder the embodiment of the church itself, as well as contribute most significantly to the formation of embodied and embedded individual congregants. Important aspects of embodied worship are the degree to which persons actively participate, rather than passively view and hear, and whether worship enhances interpersonal connectedness. Last, we discussed the nature of the caring and compassionate life of the church in terms of meeting problems of human disability. Here we particularly emphasized the difference it makes in ministering to the sick or disabled to conceive of persons as whole physical beings, while recognizing in the process our own various forms of disability and dependence. We are all, at various times in our lives and to differing degrees, disabled and dependent because we are all essentially physical beings. It is from the context of our own dependence that we are called to minister to one another within the church and to those in our communities.

WHAT WE ARE NOT SAYING

It is also important to clarify for our readers and, in some cases, to reiterate,a few things that we are *not* saying, but that people often presume we are saying or implying. First, we are not making any statements about the nature of God. To be theologically technical, we are espousing anthropological physicalism (the physical embodiment of personhood), but not universal physicalism. Scripture is clear that God is spirit – a point that we acknowledge, accept, and revere. There is mystery about the nature of God, as well as how God, as spirit, communicates with embodied human beings, but we are, nevertheless, deeply committed to spiritness as an ineffable aspect of God. Human beings, however, are entirely a part of God's physical creation, but with unique capacities to be aware of God's presence.

Secondly, we are neither biological nor environmental determinists. In spite of taking embodiment and embeddedness seriously, we do not believe that humans are "nothing but the mindless motion of molecules,"[1] nor are we merely slavish, habitual responders to life events, with our actions based solely on prior environmental conditioning and learning. These sorts of determinism would exonerate humans from personal responsibility for sin. Human persons are significantly influenced and shaped by their physiology, including genetics, and by their history of environmental interactions (for example, previous experiences of attachment and imitation), but they, nevertheless, maintain the capacity for freedom and decision making. The concept of *emergence* that we have described makes this point very clear, undermining any theory of complete determinism.[2] Out of human physiological embodiment and environmental influences, capacities emerge that allow humans to engage in novel behaviors and have new thoughts. In our freedom, we are responsible agents – but we are not as free as we sometimes like to think we are.

Third, we are not saying that subjective, inner experiences and emotions are not important in the Christian life. Rather, emotions and feelings are bodily reactions that serve the purpose of giving us information about the significance of the events, including religious events, that we are involved in, physically or in our imaginations. Thus, we encourage spiritual formational practices, such as corporate worship, prayer, devotion, and ritual, that are accompanied by subjective experiences and emotions, so long as: (1) they are recognized as totally embodied – that is, not a manifestation of an inner soul; and (2) they are understood as

---

[1] Donald M. MacKay, *Human Science and Human Dignity* (Downers Grove, IL: InterVarsity Press, 1979), 27.

[2] Human freedom within the context of physical embodiment is thoroughly defended in Nancey Murphy and Warren S. Brown, *Did My Neurons Make Me Do It? Philosophical and Neurobiological Perspectives on Moral Responsibility and Free Will* (Oxford, U.K.: Oxford University Press, 2007).

signals about the character of our current social-communal context (that is, indications of the meaning of the situation in which we find ourselves). When God, as spirit, moves upon human bodies and church bodies, it is often signaled to us by our bodily reactions. The problem is that emotions are easily manipulated, which may cause us to misunderstand their contextual origin and significance.

Fourth, this embodied perspective of human nature always raises questions about life after death. Our view of human nature does not imply that, since there is no soul, physical death is the end of existence. While we would not presume to make any definitive statements about the nature of life after death, we do believe it will involve bodies – resurrected, recreated, and changed bodies, but bodies, nevertheless.[3]

RETROSPECTIVE ON DUALISM

Despite our commitment to the position that persons do not have a dual nature (body and soul), we do not mean to imply that body-soul dualism represents some egregious heresy or has not had value in the historical life of the church. In fact, given that both of us were raised and nurtured as Christians within this traditional view of persons, it would be disingenuous for us to take such a position. Dualism has served some good and useful purposes within Christian thought and life. For example, it has provided impetus for a certain form of evangelism, based on the concept of souls needing to be saved. Based on concern for the status of one's own soul, the individualism inherent in dualism has served as motivation for taking seriously the call to personal faith beyond family, parish, or national or cultural membership. The inward experiential and emotive tendencies of dualism have contributed to the expressiveness of Pentecostal worship forms that have had a great impact on the modern church, both good news in its expressive and congregational joy, and, to some degree, bad news in adding momentum to our penchant toward inward, experiential spirituality. It could also be argued that the dualistic

---

[3] See N. T. Wright, *Surprised by Hope: Rethinking Heaven, the Resurrection, and the Mission of the Church* (New York: Harper Collins, 2008); and Joel B. Green, *Body, Soul, and Human Life: The Nature of Humanity in the Bible* (Grand Rapids, MI: Baker Books, 2008).

understanding of the human person leant itself to taking seriously the call to personal piety seen in many holiness traditions. This inward piety or personal holy responsibility, while in our view overly individualistic, served as an important balance to a purely social gospel that is easily disconnected from any spiritual and communal concerns, resulting in nothing but social work. However, personal piety can also contribute to an emphasis on nothing beyond a personal relationship with Christ, with little concern for other aspects of the Gospel narrative.

Notwithstanding such contributions of dualism, we believe that a shift to a wholistic view of humankind would result in a significant, positive reorganization of the church and its practices. As we have argued in this book, there is significant value to be gained by recapturing an embodied view of human nature – value in the form of a more robust understanding of Christian life. A different view of human nature entails a different outcome for Christian life.

We must all live with the caveat that we are humans with limited knowledge and are easily caught up in contemporary currents of thought or are corrupted by self-indulgent ideas and motives. Although we will never reach perfection in our understanding of the church or of ourselves, we can nevertheless know with some clarity that which represents a notable *improvement* over what we previously understood. Thus, the embodied-embedded view of others and ourselves leads us out of individualism and self-centered inwardness toward our communities, and toward God who is ever present and active in the world.

EMERGENCE AND THE CHURCH

The thought project that is represented in this book does not come *de novo* out of totally autonomous thinking by us as authors. We too are very much embedded in cultural, theological, ecclesial, and academic communities with their trends of thought and life that influence our own thinking. We trust we have contributed to pushing forward the ideas that have influenced us. However, it is worthwhile to be more explicit regarding the broader cultural, theological, and ecclesial trends of which we consider our work to be an expression.

In her book *The Great Emergence*, religion editor Phyllis Tickle[4] describes a current, ongoing upheaval in the world and the church, which she calls the Great Emergence. We believe that her description provides a reasonable representation of the wider context of the ideas we have expressed in this book. Tickle argues that approximately every 500 years the church holds a giant "rummage sale." By rummage sale she means a major upheaval, in which accumulated, unnecessary practices and ideas are jettisoned and only the most essential are kept – but enhanced by new practices and ideas. During these so-called rummage sales, the structures of institutionalized Christianity are shaken to their roots. Historically, approximately 500 years ago, the Reformation took place, involving the rise of Protestantism and denominationalism; approximately 500 years before that was the Great Schism when Eastern Orthodox and Western Roman Catholicism split; and roughly 500 years before that was the period of the Great Decline and Fall of Rome, involving also the Ecumenical Council of Chalcedon, the "clean-up" of the church by Pope Gregory I, and the schism with Oriental Orthodoxy. Tickle argues that these ecclesial rummage sales were concurrent with political, economic, and social upheavals (for example, the fall of Rome or the Renaissance). Changes in the church are inseparable from, or influenced by, events happening in the surrounding culture.

These upheavals are broad in their impact on the church. Tickle suggests that there are three major results of this kind of rummage sale:

First, a new, more vital form of Christianity does indeed emerge. Second, the organized expression of Christianity which up until then had been the dominant one is reconstituted into a more pure and less ossified expression of its former self. As a result of this usually energetic but rarely benign process, the Church actually ends up with two new creatures where once there had been only one. That is, in the course of birthing a brand-new expression of its faith and praxis, the Church also gains a grand refurbishment of the older one. The third result is of equal, if not greater, significance, though. That is, every time the incrustations of an overly established Christianity have been broken open, the faith has spread – and been spread – dramatically into new geographic and demographic areas, thereby

[4] Phyllis Tickle, *The Great Emergence: How Christianity is Changing and Why* (Grand Rapids, MI: Baker Books, 2008).

increasing exponentially the range and depth of Christianity's reach as a result of its time of unease and distress.[5]

Tickle's point is that the emergence of a new form of Christianity is beneficial to the older version as well – the newer version forces the older version to transform. So, as Protestantism emerged as a new form of Christianity, Roman Catholicism was forced to make changes to its structures and practices, the result of which was to advance its message in the world.

According to Tickle, we are now in the midst of another rummage sale, the Great Emergence. This upheaval is represented conceptually by a number of "posts": post-modern (a change with respect to our understanding of truth), post-denominational (denominational differences have significantly less meaning to most Christians), post-Christendom (with respect to the aims and objectives of mission and evangelism), and even post-Christian (at least so far as the predominance of Christianity within Western culture).

One of the many outcomes of this upheaval has been that the designation "Christian" has come to be viewed more as a center toward which persons progressively move, than as a boundary that must be crossed. Another part of this upheaval is the flattening of hierarchy and a deep distrust of institutionalism in the church. With less concern over denominations, institutions, and hierarchy, the new churches of the Great Emergence tend to be small and self-organizing (which Tickle compares to the self-organization of an anthill, similar to our own use of that metaphor). This is also coupled with a tendency to be more communal, emphasizing values of authenticity and conversation. Apparently, what is not being sold in this rummage sale is tradition – there is commitment "to perpetuate the tradition and not the institution."[6] For those affected by the Great Emergence, but choosing to stay within denominational churches, Tickle talks about the "hyphenateds," such as "Presby-mergents or Metho-mergents or Luther-mergents."[7] The impact on these hyphenateds within traditional denominations

---

[5] Tickle, p. 17.
[6] Phyllis Tickle, "Like an Anthill," an interview in *Faith & Leadership*, http://www.faithandleadership.com/multimedia/phyllis-tickle-anthill.
[7] Tickle, "Like an Anthill."

makes it clear that the sometimes controversial "emergent church" is merely one part of a much larger cultural and ecclesiastical movement of emergence.

Consistent with our previous description of the church as a dynamical system, the Great Emergence can be viewed as a response to a cultural catastrophe that is dynamically reforming the body that is the church. Social, economic, scientific, and conceptual changes present the church with new challenges that have pushed the church into disequilibrium. Major upheaval is provoking a reorganization of the church that Tickle sees as a rummage sale. Those churches that are less rigid and open to change are reforming (emerging), but others are resisting by rigidly trying to maintain the status quo.

Of particular relevance to our book is Tickle's suggestion that one of the cultural influences that is advancing the Great Emergence in contemporary Western Christianity is the question of the "self." She suggests, as we have done in this book, that advances in biology, psychology, anthropology, neuroscience, and cognitive science have forced us to ask essential questions about what it means to be human: What is it that makes humans human? It is into this discussion that we have entered with an argument for a more embodied and socially embedded understanding of humankind within Christian theology and practice. This new – but really quite old – understanding of the human person as a body, not a body inhabited by a soul, is an important conceptual revision that should emerge from the rummage sale currently happening in the church.

POSTSCRIPT

We end this book with an emphasis on the tradition and belief that must be preserved in whatever emerges – the image of the embodied Christ, who forgave sins, healed bodies, and fostered interpersonal relationships characterized by kindness, justice, peace, and reconciliation. We understand Jesus' ministry as both the reconciliation of humans to God and a continuation of the prophets' call for justice for all people – all bodies! Jesus frequently engaged in scathing social commentary, making it clear that embodied and socially embedded ministry in a physical world is at the heart of the Gospel. This ministry will not be realized by autonomous, individual Christians or by a one-dimensional and pale Christianity with no other call than to personal relationships with Jesus. The Kingdom of God will only come to ultimate fruition through the Body of Christ – the outcome of a truly embodied and embedded faith. It is this Body that continually forms human bodies into some measure of Christlikeness. And it is through the power of the Holy Spirit, operating in and through bodily persons who are deeply embedded in church bodies, that we can imagine why Jesus could say, "Very truly I tell you, whoever believes in me will do the works I have been doing, and they will do even greater things than these, because I am going to the Father" (John 14:12, NIV).

Selected Resources

Balswick, Jack O., Pamela Ebstyne King, and Kevin S. Reimer. *The Reciprocating Self: Human Development in Theological Perspective*. Illinois: IVP, 2005.

Bargh, John A. and Tanya L. Chartrand. "The Unbearable Automaticity of Being." *American Psychologist* 54, 7 (1999).

Berry, Wendell. "The Body and the Earth," in Wendell Berry, *Recollected Essays*. San Francisco: Northpoint Press, 1981.

Bloom, Harold. *The American Religion: The Emergence of the Post-Christian Nation*. New York: Simon and Schuster, 1992.

Bowlby, John. *Attachment and Loss*: Vol. 1. *Attachment*. New York: Basic Books, 1969.; Vol. 2. *Separation: Anxiety and Anger*. New York: Basic Books, 1973.; Vol. 3. *Loss: Sadness and* Depression. New York: Basic Books, 1980.

Brown, Ramond E. *An Introduction to the New Testament*. New York: Doubleday, 1997.

Brown, Warren S., Nancey Murphy, and H. Newton Malony, eds. *Whatever Happened of the Soul? Scientific and Theological Portraits of Human Nature*. Minneapolis: Fortress Press, 1998.

Brown, Warren S., Sarah D. Marion, and Brad Strawn. "Human Relationality, Spiritual Formation, and Wesleyan Communities," in M. K. Armistead, B. Strawn, and R. Wright, eds. *Wesleyan Theology and Social Science: The Dance of Practical Divinity and Discovery*. Tyne: Cambridge Scholars Publishing, 2010, 95–112.

Brown, Warren S. "Human Nature, Physicalism, Spirituality, and Healing: Theological Views of a Neuroscientist." *Ex Auditu* 21 (2005):112–127.

Cassidy, Jude and Phillip R. Shaver, eds. *Handbook of Attachment: Theory, Research, and Clinical Implications*. New York: Guilford Press, 1999.

Clapp, Rodney. *Tortured Wonders: Christian Spirituality for People, Not Angels*. MI: Baker, 2004.

Curtiss, Susan. *Genie: A Psycholinguistic Study of a Modern-Day "Wild Child."* Boston: Academic Press, 1977.

Damasio, Antonio. *Descartes' Error: Emotion, Reason, and the Human Brain*. Boston: Norton, 1994.

Deacon, Terrance. *The Symbolic Species: The Co-evolution of Language and the Brain*. New York, W. W. Norton & Co., 1997.

Girard, René. *Things Hidden since the Foundation of the World*. Stanford, CA: Stanford University Press, 1978.

Green, Joel B. *Body, Soul and Human Life: The Nature of Humanity in the Bible*. Grand Rapids, MI: Baker Academic, 2008.

Green, Joel B. "Three Exegetical Forays into the Body-Soul Distinction." *Criswell Theological Review* 7, 2 (Spring 2010):3–18.

Green, Joel B., ed. *What About the Soul? Neuroscience and Christian Anthropology*. Nashville: Abington Press, 2004.

Gunton, Colin E. *Christ and Creation*. Grand Rapids, MI: Wm B. Eerdmans, 1992.

Hauerwas, Stanley. *A Community of Character: Toward a Constructive Christian Social Ethic*. University of Notre Dame Press, 1981.

Jeeves, Malcolm A., ed. *From Cells to Souls – and Beyond: Changing Portraits of Human Nature*. Grand Rapids, MI: Eardmans, 2004.

Jeeves, Malcolm A., ed. *Human Nature*. Edinburgh: The Royal Society of Edinburgh, 2006.

Jeeves, Malcolm A., and Warren S. Brown. *Neuroscience, Psychology and Religion: Illusions, Delusions, and Realities about Human Nature*. Radnor, PA: Templeton Press, 2009.

Johnson, Steven. *Emergence: The Connected Lives of Ants, Brains, Cities and Software*. New York: Schribner, 2001.

Juarrero, Alicia. *Dynamics in Action: Intentional Behavior as a Complex System*. Cambridge, MA: Bradford Books, 2002.

Keysers, Christian and Valeria Gazzola. "Towards a Unifying Neural Theory of Social Cognition," in S. Anders et al., eds. *Progress in Brain Research 156* (Elsevier 2006):379–401.

Lakoff, George and Mark Johnson. *Philosophy in the Flesh: The Embodied Mind and Its Challenge to Western Thought*. New York: Basic Books, 1999.

MacIntyre, Alasdair. *After Virtue: A Study in Moral Theology*, 3rd edition, Notre Dame, IN: University of Notre Dame Press, 2007.

MacIntyre, Alasdair. *Dependent Rational Animals: Why Human Beings Need the Virtues*. Chicago: Open Court, 1999.

MacKay, Donald M. *Behind the Eye*. Oxford, UK: Basil Blackwell, 1991.

Markham, Paul N. *Rewired: Exploring Religious Conversion*. Eugene, OR: Pickwick Publications, 2007.

Murphy, Nancey. *Bodies and Souls, or Spirited Bodies?* London: Cambridge, 2006.

Murphy, Nancey and Warren S. Brown. *Did My Neurons Make Me Do It? Philosophical and Neurobiological Perspectives on Moral Responsibility and Free Will*. Oxford, U.K.: Oxford University Press, 2007.

McNamare, Patrick, ed. *Where God and Science Meet*: Vol. 3: *The Psychology of Religious Experience*. Westport, CT: Praeger, 2006.

Pennebaker, James W. *Opening Up: The Healing Power of Expressing Emotions*. New York: Guilford Press, 1997.

Powell, Mark Alan. *What Do They Hear? Bridging the Gap Between Pulpit & Pew*. Nashville: Abingdon, 2007.

Powell, Samuel M., and Michael E. Lodahl, eds. *Embodied Holiness: Toward a Corporate Theology of Spiritual Growth*. Downers Grove, IL: Intervarsity Press, 1999.

Quartz, Steven and Terrence Sejnowski. *Liars, Lovers, and Heroes: What the New Brain Science Reveals About How We Become Who We Are.* New York: Quill, 2002.

Savage-Rumbaugh, Sue and Roger Lewin. *Kanzi: The Ape at the Brink of the Human Mind.* New York: Wiley, 1994.

Schore, Allan N. *Affect Regulation and the Origin of the Self: The Neurobiology of Emotional Development.* Hillsdale, NJ: Lawrance Erlbaum Associates, 1994.

Shults, F. LeRon. *Reforming Theological Anthropology: After the Philosophical Turn to Relationality.* Grand Rapids, MI: Eerdmans, 2003.

Siegel, Daniel J., and Marion F. Solomon, eds. *Healing Trauma: Attachment, Mind, Body, and Brain.* New York: W.W. Norton and Co, 2003.

Stassen, Glen H., and David P. Gushee. *Kingdom Ethics: Following Jesus in Contemporary Context.* Downers Grove, IL: Intervarsity Press, 2003.

Stern, Daniel. *The Interpersonal World of the Infant: A View from Psychoanalysis and Developmental Psychology.* New York: Basic Books, 1985.

Thomas, Owen. "Interiority and Christian spirituality," *The Journal of Religion* 80, no. 1 (2000).

Wallin, David J. *Attachment in Psychotherapy.* New York: Guildford, 2007.

Welker, Michael. "We Live Deeper Than We Think: The Genius of Schleiermacher's Earliest Ethics," *Theology Today* 56, no. 2 (1999).

Wright, N. T. *Surprised by Hope: Rethinking Heaven, the Resurrection, and the Mission of the Church.* New York: Harper One, 2008.

Wright, N. T. *The New Testament and the People of God.* Minneapolis: Fortress Press, 1992.

Yalom, Irving. *The Theory and Practice of Group Psychotherapy,* 5th ed., New York: Basic Books, 2005.

Young, Kay and Jeffrey L. Saver. "The Neurology of Narrative," *Substance: A Review of Theory & Literary Criticism* 30, 2001, Issue 1/2, 2001, 78.

Index

change: personal transformation and hope for, 91–2; personal transformation and models of, 98–100. *See also* openness; personhood; spiritual formation
character: formation of, 53–5, 58–9, 64, 69, 143, 152; of groups and churches, 131–3, 139, 141, 152
Chemel, Benjamin R., 44n24
children, development of: disorders of, 67–9; and empathy, 63–4; and formation of personhood, 69–70; and imitation, 56–8; and interpersonal attachment, 59–63; and language, 64–7; openness and self-organization in, 53–5; and shared attention, 58–9; and social experiences, 52–3, 68–9; and Von Economo neurons, 37
Christianity: disability and concept of body in, 153–7; emergence of new form of, 165–7; and formation of personhood in children, 69; Gnosticism in contemporary, 23–7; and image of embodied Christ,167–8;; maturation and formation of wisdom and virtue, 87; purposes of dualism within thought and life of, 163–4; questions raised concerning Christian life, 9; spiritual formation and imitation of Christ, 115–18. *See also* Bible; Body of Christ; church; conversion; God
church: as alternative narrative, 142–7; anticipatory expectations and destructive relational cycles in, 90–1; Body of Christ and definition of, 130–1, 160–1; catastrophe and growth of, 131–5; and "church growth," 118–19; and "church shopper," 106–107; and concept of emergence, 164–7; disability and Christian formation in, 153–7; dualism in early, 22–3; as dynamic network, 123–4, 125–7; and embodied worship, 147–52, 161; and embodiment of personhood of children in programs, 69–70; and group size, 135–9; growth of into Body of Christ, 9; implications of views on spirituality and the body for, 7–8; leadership and self-organization of, 127–31; nature of as social system or network, 122; overview of perspectives on human beings as bodies in context of, 8–9; physical life of, 157; quantity and quality of communication
in, 125; reasons for attending, 106–108; and reciprocal nature of system formation, 125–7; and role of secure attachment in spiritual formation, 113–15; small groups within setting of, 94; and social formation of persons, 110–11; and spiritual formation, 108–10, 118–20; and stories, 133, 141. *See also* Christianity; Protestantism; Roman Catholicism
"church growth," 118–19
"church shopper," 106–107
cities, and self-organization, 127–8
clinical psychology, 89
cognitive disability, 155
Colossians 1:27 (NIV), 109
communication, and formation of bodies, 124–5
community: and goal of church, 7–8; and spiritual formation as purpose of church, 110. *See also* neighborhood
complex dynamical systems, theory of, 74, 78
consequences, and stories, 143–4
conversion: spiritual formation and purpose of church, 108, 109; stories about dramatic and sudden, 72
1 Corinthians 4:15–17, 115; 15:35–58, 21
2 Corinthians 5:1–6, 21
corporate worship, 147, 150
cosmological dualism, 20
culture: and catastrophe as source of growth for church, 134–5; and Great Emergence in contemporary Christianity, 167; and interpretation of stories, 144. *See also* Greek culture; ethnicity; Native Americans

Damasio, Antonio, 40
Deacon, Terrence, 65–6
demographics, changes in as source of catastrophe, 135
dendrites, and memory systems, 73
dependence, and disability, 153–4
DePree, Max, 145
Descartes, René, 15–16, 20, 21, 26, 30, 32, 38, 47
desire, and process of imitation, 58, 79, 81–2
determinism, and concept of emergence, 162
development. *See* children; personhood
dilemmas, and morality, 39–41
disorganized attachment, 60–1, 64
Down's syndrome, 155
Doystoyevsky, Fyodor, 42–3
drugs, and religious experiences, 44–5. *See also* substance abuse
dualism: and Bible's lessons on human nature, 16–22; in early church, 22–3; explanation of concept, 5–6, 14; history of, 14–16; and issues of illness and disability, 156; and models of change, 99; overview of discussions on, 8, 11–12;

dualism (cont.)
  purposes of within Christian thought
    and life, 163–4; and salvation, 109; and
    view of self, 13–14
Dunbar, Robin, 136–7
dynamical systems: ant colony as example
    of, 74–5; catastrophe and growth or
    change in, 131; and church as dynamic
    network, 123–4, 125–7; and openness
    to change, 112
dysnarrativia, 84

economics, as source of chaos and
    catastrophe, 135
Ecumenical Council of Chalcedon, 165
electromagnetic stimulation, and religious
    experiences, 44
embodiment: and image of embodied Christ,
    167–8; of personhood in church
    programs for children, 69–70; and
    monism, 5; and personal
    transformation, 99–100; and
    predominant modern view of
    spirituality, 2–4; and spiritual
    formation, 109–10; of worship in
    church, 147–52, 161. See also body
emergence: church and concept of, 164–7; of
    complex self-organizing communities,
    127–8, 129–31, 142; of human
    properties and capacities, 6, 30, 49, 54,
    69, 74; and role of church in Christian
    faith, 122; and role of worship in
    formation of church as body, 149; and
    theory of complete determinism, 162
emotions: and moral intuitions, 40–1; and
    worship, 148–9
empathy: and child development, 63–4, 66;
    and language, 66; neuroscience and
    research on, 34–5
enmeshment, and group size, 138
environmental determinism, 162
epilepsy, and religious experiences, 29, 43
ethical behavior, and role of language in child
    development, 4, 25, 66, 157. See also
    morality
ethnicity, and cultural difference as source of
    catastrophe, 135
Eucharist, and worship life of church
    congregations, 151, 152
evangelism, and dualism, 163

family: catastrophe and change or growth in,
    131–3; as dynamical system, 123–4,
    125; and reciprocity, 126; and self-
    organization, 128
frontal lobe, of brain, 33–4, 40, 46, 54
functional MRI (fMRI), 31, 64

Galen of Pergamum, 15
Gazzola, Valeria, 56n12
Genesis, 2, 17
Girard, René, 81, 117
glossolalia, 46
Gnosticism: and concept of body and soul, 5;
    in contemporary Christianity, 23–7,
    107–108, 109; and early church, 22;
    and issues of illness and disability, 155
God: nature of, 161–2; spirituality as ongoing
    relationship with, 7
"God module," in brain, 43
Good Friday experiment, 45
Good Samaritan story, 143
Granqvist, P., 44n23
Great Emergence, 165–7
Great Schism, 165
Greek culture, influence on Palestine at time
    of Jesus, 15
Green, Joel, 6n3, 18, 19n10, 20, 21
Greene, Joshua, 39
Gregory I, Pope, 165
group contagion, 115–16
groups: churches and size of, 135–9, 152;
    processes of personal transformation in
    small, 92–4, 117. See also
    psychotherapy
Gushee, David, 25–6

hallucinogens, and religious experiences,
    44–5
Hauerwas, Stanley, 4, 146
health and wealth story, 119
Hebrews 6:12; 13:7, 115
hope, and change in individuals, 91–3
human nature: and concept of *having* or *being*
    a body, 4–5; embodied perspective of
    and questions about life after death, 163;
    and models of change, 99; neuroscience
    and distinctive characteristics of, 29–30;
    and relationality, 33; and social
    embeddedness of persons, 5–6;
    teachings of Bible about, 16–22

identity, stories and construction of, 144–5
imagination, stories and regulation of, 146
imitation: and child development, 56–8, 59;
    of Christ and spiritual formation,
    115–18; in formation of personhood
    and unconsciousness, 78–82
immediacy, and group therapy, 93, 98
individualism, and dualism, 15, 24–7, 163
infants, social experiences and development
    of, 52
"In the Garden" (hymn), 151
inhibited temperament, 55
insecure attachment, 60, 61, 62, 77, 113

trust, neuroscience and study of development of, 35

unconscious habits, good and bad of, 89–91
universality, and process of change, 93, 98

virtue, and formation of personhood, 85–7
Von Economo neurons, 36–7, 41

Welker, Michael, 116–17

Whiten, Andrew, 33
wisdom, and formation of personhood, 85–7
worship: embodiment of in church, 147–52, 161; and *experiences* versus *services*, 107; Pentecostal forms of, 163; solitary forms of, 111
Wright, N. T., 6n3, 16–17, 19–20

Yalom, Irving, 92–3, 94, 98, 117
Young, Kay, 84